Junior College _____ of St. Louis
Library
4386 Lindell Boulevard
St. Louis 8, Missouri

PRINTED IN U.S.A.

THE
du Ponts

THE
du Ponts

From Gunpowder to Nylon

by **MAX DORIAN**

TRANSLATED BY EDWARD B. GARSIDE

With Photographs by
Dixie Reynolds

Little, Brown and Company · Boston · Toronto

A shorter version of this work was published in Paris by
Librairie Plon in the "History of Great Enterprises" series,
under the title *Du Pont de Nemours: De la Poudre au Nylon.*

Published simultaneously in Canada
by Little, Brown & Company (Canada) Limited

PRINTED IN THE UNITED STATES OF AMERICA

Acknowledgments

The author is extremely grateful to the staff of the former Longwood Library (now the Eleutherian Mills Historical Library), who helped to find and identify numerous unpublished documents and manuscripts which were invaluable in laying the foundations of this book. He would like to add that without the collaboration of Dixie Reynolds this volume would not have been possible. To her and to them he can only say: *"Merci."*

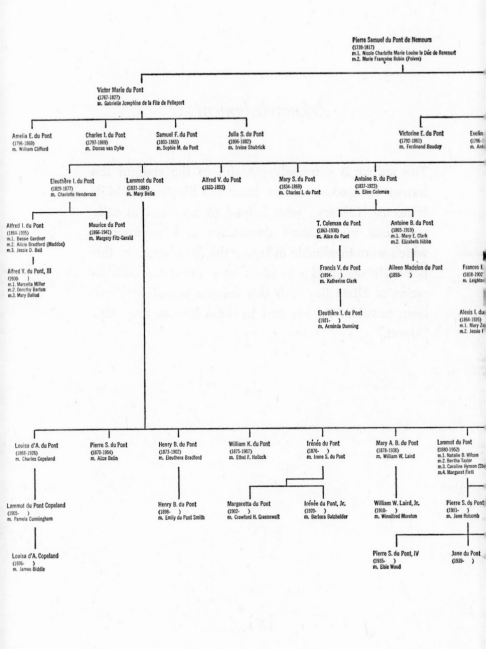

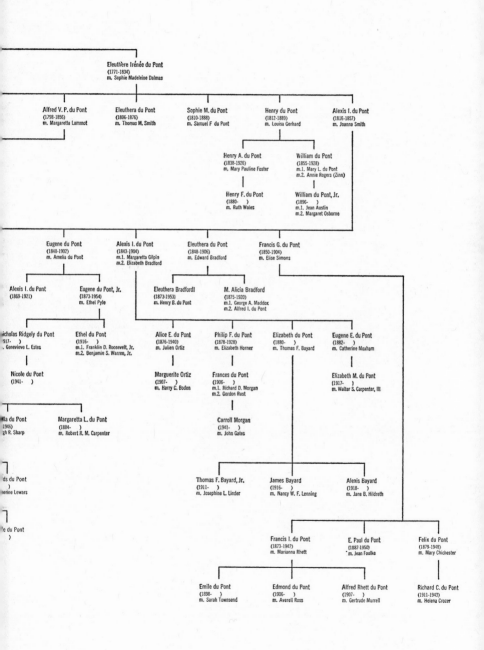

Eleuthère Irénée du Pont
(1771-1834)
m. Sophie Madeleine Dalmas

Alfred V. P. du Pont
(1798-1856)
m. Margaretta Lammot

Eleuthera du Pont
(1806-1876)
m. Thomas M. Smith

Sophie M. du Pont
(1810-1888)
m. Samuel F. du Pont

Henry du Pont
(1812-1889)
m. Louisa Gerhard

Alexis I. du Pont
(1816-1857)
m. Joanna Smith

Henry A. du Pont
(1838-1926)
m. Mary Pauline Foster

William du Pont
(1855-1928)
m.1. Mary L. du Pont
m.2. Annie Rogers (Zinn)

Henry F. du Pont
(1880-   )
m. Ruth Wales

William du Pont, Jr.
(1896-   )
m.1. Jean Austin
m.2. Margaret Osborne

Eugene du Pont
(1840-1902)
m. Amelia du Pont

Alexis I. du Pont
(1843-1904)
m.1. Margaretta Gilpin
m.2. Elizabeth Bradford

Eleuthera du Pont
(1848-1906)
m. Edward Bradford

Francis G. du Pont
(1850-1904)
m. Elise Simons

Alexis I. du Pont
(1869-1921)

Eugene du Pont, Jr.
(1873-1954)
m. Ethel Pyle

Eleuthera Bradford
(1873-1953)
m. Henry B. du Pont

M. Alicia Bradford
(1875-1920)
m.1. George A. Maddox
m.2. Alfred I. du Pont

icholas Ridgely du Pont
(1917-   )
. Genevieve L. Estes

Ethel du Pont
(1916-   )
m.1. Franklin D. Roosevelt, Jr.
m.2. Benjamin S. Warren, Jr.

Alice E. du Pont
(1876-1940)
m. Julien Ortiz

Philip F. du Pont
(1878-1928)
m. Elizabeth Horner

Elizabeth du Pont
(1880-   )
m. Thomas F. Bayard

Eugene E. du Pont
(1882-   )
m. Catherine Moxham

Nicole du Pont
(1941-   )

Marguerite Ortiz
(1907-   )
m. Harry C. Boden

Frances du Pont
(1906-   )
m.1. Richard D. Morgan
m.2. Gordon Rust

Elizabeth M. du Pont
(1917-   )
m. Walter S. Carpenter, III

la du Pont
1946)
gh R. Sharp

Margaretta L. du Pont
(1884-   )
m. Robert R. M. Carpenter

Carroll Morgan
(1941-   )
m. John Gates

ds du Pont
)
erine Lewars

Thomas F. Bayard, Jr.
(1911-   )
m. Josephine L. Linder

James Bayard
(1916-   )
m. Nancy W. F. Lenning

Alexis Bayard
(1918-   )
m. Jane B. Hildreth

e du Pont
)

Francis I. du Pont
(1873-1942)
m. Marianna Rhett

E. Paul du Pont
(1887-1950)
m. Jean Foulke

Felix du Pont
(1879-1948)
m. Mary Chichester

Emile du Pont
(1898-   )
m. Sarah Townsend

Edmond du Pont
(1906-   )
m. Averell Ross

Alfred Rhett du Pont
(1907-   )
m. Gertrude Murrell

Richard C. du Pont
(1911-1943)
m. Helena Crozer

Contents

Illustrations

[xi]

THE
du Ponts

1

The Physiocrat and His Children

The expected arrival from France of Mr. du Pont de Nemours cannot but excite the liveliest emotions in the minds of such of our people as are sensible to his own land and more especially to this country in arranging the late Peace. . . .

GEORGE WASHINGTON
November 9, 1799

O F ALL THE FRENCH CITIES so rich in an ancient past, La Rochelle is least changed by the passage of the years. The American descendants of the Huguenots who forsook La Rochelle after the revocation of the Edict of Nantes by Louis XIV in 1685, and who founded New Rochelle in the state of New York, today find the old section in the mother-city looking almost as it did in ancestral times.

La Rochelle lies on the Atlantic coast about halfway between Paris and the Spanish border, protected against

[3]

the fury of the Atlantic by the islands of Ré, Aix and Oléron. Two sturdy crenellated towers still guard its inner harbor, while yet another, the ancient lighthouse, Gothic and slender, dominates the ramparts.

Here the wars of religion left more of a mark than the Revolution of 1789. Unlike what happened in cities in the Bordeaux area, and above all in the area of Nantes, popular emancipation was effected in La Rochelle without giving rise to excesses. This was probably because the *noblesse d'épée* — the ancient nobility of warrior origin — had never played much of a role here. Also, it was a long while before the mob's wrath turned on the bourgeoisie, in large measure Protestant, which had at first pinned its hopes on the new order. In 1799, ten years after the fall of the Bastille, the desire of the La Rochelle citizens, and of the Rochelais middle class in particular, was to restore a peaceful climate favorable to business as usual. However, even under the relatively moderate régime of the Directoire, a return to times of peace seemed far off to these bourgeois. They felt this more than inlanders, since they could see, rotting in the muddy dockside waters, abandoned merchant ships long immobilized by the blockade of the French coast. Right in their own snug basin, neutral American ships with decaying hulls and sails were visible evidence that the war with the outside world was still in progress. These American vessels, and others falsely carrying the American flag, had been seized at sea by privateers of the Republic on suspicion of trafficking with the British.

And it was precisely because of the presence of these American vessels that early in May, 1799, a stranger descended from the Paris stagecoach. His attire betrayed an elegance that a few years before might have been suspect. His passport, handed over to the police for identification, revealed that the stranger's name was Victor du Pont, that he was thirty-two years old, five feet, ten inches tall, and had "light brown hair, an oval face, a short nose and large eyes." The declared purpose of his journey was to carry out affairs of a business nature. Victor du Pont kept to himself the fact that he was secretly charged by Citizen Talleyrand, Foreign Minister of the Directoire, to obtain exact information about the number and condition of American crews awaiting authorization to go back to sea with their vessels.

Talleyrand was clearly aware that unless he had these ships released, relations of the French Directoire with the American government would continue to be strained and would perhaps worsen. As a shrewd statesman, he wanted to ease the situation. However, it was difficult for the Directoire to annul decrees which permitted French privateers to pursue neutral vessels in the smuggling trade. But Talleyrand decided that by use of tact and discretion a plan could be worked out to effect the release of at least those American vessels for which there was no clear proof of dereliction. Victor du Pont was just the man Talleyrand needed to carry out this mission, because du Pont had a personal interest in its success.

On May 22 Victor, no longer a stranger in La Rochelle, wrote his father:

> *La Rochelle, 3 Prairial, Year VII [May 22, 1799]*
> *Mon cher Papa,*
> *I found here your two letters from Rotterdam, dated the 17 and 20 Floréal, and have since learned with much pleasure that you are back home in good health with your traveling companion.*
> *I have received many kindnesses from your old friend M. de Richemont and M. Trouard, a most interesting and amiable man to whom Irénée gave me a letter of introduction. But neither the one nor the other, nor any merchant in this city, at least judging by the general state of mind and financial condition, offers much hope (at least for the time being) of making my stay here useful to the Company, nor do any connections I might [otherwise] be able to make here. . . . La Rochelle has suffered several bankruptcies which have rocked the whole financial community. They had outfitted many privateers here which have been captured, as well as some of the shipments attempted under the Danish and Prussian flags, all lost to the British thanks to the bad faith of the captains. The majority of the business peo-*

ple for this reason have neither the means nor the desire
to keep trying, but are waiting for peace. It has appeared in the local newspapers that on an English letter
of marque an order has been found to stop all neutral
vessels leaving France. . . . That alone is enough to
ruin our plans. It has been useless for me to tell anyone
that our house would be interested in obtaining consignments. I repeat to you, I have no hope for anything. It might not be difficult to find buyers for our
shares, general as the discouragement may be, were
not capital proportionately scarce. . . .

When I have finished the survey of the Brooks vessel
and estimated the repairs she needs, and after I have
lined up some future cargoes for us, I will go to Rochefort and from there to Oléron, and afterwards may be
able to go to Bordeaux before returning here in accord-
ance with whatever instructions you give me.

Coming down here from the North, I spent two days
with a judge, a worthy man whom I got to know
through Regnault [de Saint-Jean-d'Angely?]. He has a
profitably situated country property. . . . His principal
income comes from brandy. He has promised me to
send a cargo with us, with one of his sons as agent in
charge, fifteen days after peace is signed. He is a man
who will keep his word, and there would be surety,
pleasure and profit in doing business with him. His
name is la Bouterie, and I shall see him again on my
way back.

I will have to have some Company certificates, some stock receipts and a résumé of the prospectus, very short, without details, containing only the general idea of the means, resources, projects, plans and hopes of our Company. . . . I will show it to those I think disposed to take one or two shares from me in exchange for being the local correspondents of our New York and Virginia offices; but, as I have already said, I am not hoping for big commissions here until the peace, and, all things considered, there is no need for us to be distressed about it, because we are not in any case too well prepared to execute them. We will need time to get set up over there; and it is enough that they should believe we have several affairs on the fire, so that everybody will be wanting to do business with us when times are more propitious. . . . I regard our project as saved and on the right track in view of the fact that we have enough capital to ensure us credit and a reputation which is greatly enhanced by your name.

Our departure is certain, our establishment over there a sure thing, and our future success there beyond doubt, but we must realize that under such difficult circumstances our first steps should be very cautious and that it will be better to make sure of two consignments coming later on in better times than to get one right away which, if it should miscarry through forces beyond our control, would redound so much the more to our discredit.

*. . . I am fairly well satisfied with what I have ac-
complished. I think I have pretty well caught on to the
jargon and charlatanism of the trade. In a word, I am
doing my best to give a good impression of our company.*

*We have here a choice of two excellent American
vessels which could take us across, the one owned by
Brooks and the other by Okinner[?]. They will be ready
about August or September. Our resources and our
friends' will have to be concentrated on them. No others
can be considered because of the problem of crews to
man them. . . .*

Je vous embrasse
avec tendresse
V. du PONT

The du Ponts, as we see, were getting ready to leave
for the United States. Not surreptitiously, like those
émigrés who were fleeing abroad to escape massacre
after their property had been seized by the government, but openly. The Directoire saw no harm in letting anyone quit France who wanted to do so.

It was a simple matter for Victor, back in Paris, to
obtain from Talleyrand's office the documents needed
to permit the *American Eagle,* owned and commanded
by Captain Brooks, to leave La Rochelle, as well as the
authorization for the du Ponts to cross the Atlantic on
this vessel. However, the craft herself had to be made

seaworthy. This was no easy task, since she had been seriously damaged by her long stay in port. Major repairs would have to be made, but Brooks had not the money to pay for them, nor was any moneylender in the city inclined to run the risk of making a loan without guarantees. As a result, the Captain had to content himself with making only those repairs which were indispensable if he was to get his vessel under sail at all. He had hoped at the very least to locate a profitable cargo, but was unable to do so for the reasons described in Victor's letter to his father. Thus he ended up having to take on a cargo of salt just big enough to permit him to buy provisions for the voyage and to accommodate, at a modest price, other passengers besides the du Ponts. He had agreed to take the du Pont family at a cheap price, in payment of his debt of gratitude for the sailing permit.

All told, Brooks had forty-two passengers on board, while the du Ponts had expected to be alone. This was far too many to permit even a decent crossing. The du Pont group, arriving at La Rochelle unaware of the Captain's difficulties, could not turn back. They went on board . . . thirteen in all. There were Pierre-Samuel and his two sons Victor and Eleuthère-Irénée, his two daughters-in-law and their five small children, followed by Mme. Bureaux de Pusy, daughter of Pierre-Samuel's second wife, with her baby, and Charles Dalmas, brother of Eleuthère-Irénée's wife.

On October 2 the *American Eagle* weighed anchor. At the beginning, the adventure was fortunate in that the vessel was not stopped for inspection by the English. But thereafter it came close to having a tragic ending. The crossing was not completed until December 31. What happened during the interim the du Ponts were to retain as a frightful memory as long as they lived. Mme. Victor du Pont (who loved to commit her impressions to paper and whose rough draft of a novel called "La Réserve Indienne" is preserved in the du Pont library at Hagley) has left us this colorful description:

Three months elapsed before this horrible and most dangerous of voyages came to an end and we finally saw the ship come to anchor — or, better said, it was her last gasp ["*ancre de salut*"] — in sight of the little town of Newport where Victor and I were landing for the second time. I am not the least tempted to introduce a shipboard diary here under the cover of these memoirs, however curious certain items might be. Numerous as our family was, it did not, unhappily, constitute a majority among the passengers. Our vessel (alas, it was cheapness alone which had induced us to take it), after its having been condemned and having languished for more than two years in La Rochelle, had, thanks to Victor's urgent solicitations — worse luck for us — been returned to its captain, who had no money to repair and renew it. He ingeniously supplied this deficiency by taking on salt and any number of passengers. This salt melted away by the minute, thanks to the water that we shipped; and then the food supply began to run low, the passengers to quarrel among themselves, the sailors to break into our trunks. The captain was unhappy about all these matters, but particularly unhappy because he didn't even know our location.* Had it not been for the one English ship and later a second who let us know where we were and who gave us food, unquestionably we would have perished almost in sight of port.

Mme. du Pont could have added that they were again fortunate that these were only merchant ships.

The thirteen du Ponts who arrived at Newport on December 31, 1799, had gone through some terrible ordeals. They had suffered cold and hunger and only by luck had escaped the worst. No matter; eight days after her arrival, Mme. Victor du Pont wrote to her friend Mme. Manigault in Charleston: "If money owed us is paid off in Philadelphia, which seems certain, what we are taking with us will be more than enough to ensure our well-being, and, if we are lucky, a large fortune for our children." This dauntless lady had the gift of prophecy.

A family tradition has it that what saved the du Ponts was that they had brought along with them, just in case, an enormous pâté, the recipe for which came from Sophie du Pont, charming and practical young wife of Eleuthère-Irénée. But whether they were saved

* A play on words not easily translated: "Le capitaine était malheureux sur tous les points, particulièrement dans *son* point."

by this pâté, or by the victuals which came in the nick
of time from the English ships who aided them near the
American coast, all the du Ponts were miserably fam-
ished and numb with cold when they went ashore at
Newport.

Everything seems worth noting in the history of the
du Ponts. Even the fact that, as Protestants, they made
La Rochelle, bastion of European Calvinism, their point
of departure, and that, furthermore, they made Newport their point of arrival, a city which the "gilded"
(*chrysogène*) aristocracy, to use Chateaubriand's words,
was to make into a millionaires' seaside resort after
1900.

The du Ponts' arrival in America, as unostentatious
as it may have been, nevertheless did not go unnoticed.
On January 7, the Newport *Journal* announced: "On
the 2nd the sloop *American Eagle* of Boston, Samuel
Brooks, captain, arrived here after taking three months
to come from the Isle of Ré. . . . The liberation of this
vessel was brought about through the efforts of Mr.
Victor du Pont, whose devotion to American interests
in France deserves the gratitude of all Americans." And
on January 18, the Philadelphia *Gazette* wrote: "We
learn from a good source . . . that Mr. du Pont, formerly French consul in Charleston [the reference was,
of course, to Victor], has arrived in New York, coming
there from Newport. It is not known whether Mr. du
Pont is charged with some official communication from

his government, but it is thought that he and those accompanying him intend to find in our country the tranquility banished from Europe. . . ."

It is obvious the editor of this newspaper believed that the du Pont family had left France after the 18th Brumaire (November 9), date of a coup d'état, and that in consequence Victor was possibly bringing with him a communication from the new government. But as we know, when Victor left France, the new Consular régime did not yet exist.

The very day that the du Ponts left La Rochelle, October 2, 1799, General Bonaparte had succeeded in running the British blockade on board the frigate *Muiron,* and had arrived from Egypt at Ajaccio in his native Corsica. Some days later he landed at Fréjus, not far from Cannes. On the 9th of November the discredited Directoire collapsed and a Consular system of government paved the way for Napoleon's coming.

Understandably, this same editor was also unaware of the fact that the du Ponts' first meal on American soil was taken by stealth. But it was not long before Pierre-Samuel himself was recounting with boyish pleasure the circumstances of this little escapade.

According to him, having left the boat as quickly as possible on their arrival in Newport on New Year's Eve, the du Ponts arrived in front of an inviting house. They knocked, but no one seemed to be at home. No doubt at church services, they assumed. Looking through the

windows, they saw by the firelight that these folks before leaving had made preparations for a midnight re-
past. The table was laid, the meal cooked and a huge
fire roared in the big fireplace. The du Ponts went inside to get warm, in the hope, one may guess, that the
owners would soon return home, whereupon they could
explain the situation and an invitation to supper would
very likely follow. Time passed. Nobody came. Temptation becoming too great, they sampled the dishes. They
tasted so good that, going from one to the other with
avid eyes and empty stomachs, they soon devoured the
whole meal. To keep on waiting after this would have
led to an impossible encounter. Pierre-Samuel and his
family decided that the sensible thing was to disappear
immediately. The Americans must have puzzled a long
time over those French pieces of gold which the honest
but indiscreet du Ponts had left beside their empty
plates.

Pierre-Samuel could have kept this incident as a
family secret, but he belonged to a generation which
made a virtue of admitting its transgressions. Such was
the generation of Jean-Jacques Rousseau, who confessed to stealing pears, and George Washington, of
cherry tree fame. Each period has its manners. Pierre-
Samuel did no more than follow them. . . .

Pierre-Samuel du Pont was born in 1739. His father
was a watchmaker, his mother belonged to the noble

but impoverished family of Montchanin, originally from Burgundy.

After getting a good education at a private boarding school run by a reputable teacher, Pierre-Samuel turned his hand to various handicrafts, thus putting the popular new theories of Jean-Jacques Rousseau into practice. He even studied medicine at a charity hospital in Paris. But these varied activities had not prevented him from writing, for he was most anxious to make a name for himself. He must have known, too, that in this eighteenth century writing had become a lucrative profession. One of his mother's cousins, the Chevalier de Jaucourt, intimate friend of such celebrated writers as Condillac, Mably and Montesquieu, obligingly agreed to read his essays. Jaucourt judged them to be so promising that he urged Pierre-Samuel to keep on and at the same time personally introduced him to d'Alembert and Diderot. Jaucourt was busy collaborating on the *Encyclopédie*. In no time at all, his young cousin found himself at home among the leading Encyclopedists. These writers ruled the salons; the Parisians were endlessly interested in their personalities, their work and their quarrels.

Through his mother's side Pierre-Samuel was distantly related to the poet de Voisenon, Abbé of Cour and admirer of Voltaire, and this gentleman in his turn gave the ambitious young man a push forward. Pierre-Samuel had just finished an essay about economics called: *Reflexions Sur l'Écrit Intitulé "La Richesse de l'État."* But he had no publisher until the Abbé found him one. This work appeared at just the right time, following as it did the same line of reasoning as the leading intellectuals of the day. In fact, it struck the right note so well that the Marquis de Mirabeau, a *grand seigneur* with considerable influence at court (not to be confused with his orator son, Honoré-Gabriel of French Revolutionary fame), looked it over on the Abbé de Voisenon's recommendation and agreed to meet the author. It was this elder Mirabeau who turned out fifty works more or less forgotten today, but is remembered for this memorable and astonishing observation: "To maintain a state of abundance in the realm, what must be done? Nothing." This declaration — plus a book he had written, *L'Economie Rurale* — had placed him in the group of economists headed by François Quesnay, personal physician to the Marquise de Pompadour. Mirabeau introduced Pierre-Samuel to Quesnay, and Quesnay in turn presented the promising young man to the ministers of Louis XV.

"I was only a child when Quesnay opened his arms to me," Pierre-Samuel was to write in his *Memoirs*. "To him I owe the warp of my spirit, the woof of which M. Turgot later was kind enough to form, work and color."

Encyclopedists, philosophers, physiocrats . . . this was the interesting milieu into which the young bourgeois Pierre-Samuel Dupont (who signed his name in this manner before he was ennobled) had just been introduced. The *Encyclopédie,* a series of large volumes published between 1750 and 1780 by a group of liberal French writers, contained the sum total of the period's knowledge and ideas. This epoch was marked by scientific curiosity — a curiosity which had first made itself felt in the ruling class. In 1769, for example, the nobility had taken a passionate interest in the development of the steam engine by James Watt. In 1776 the Marquis de Jouffroy d'Abbans was to install one of the new engines in a boat that ascended the Doubs River, and the engineer Cugnot invented another steam-powered machine to move cannon over the roads. Finally, electricity was to become the rage. King Louis XV was greatly entertained by experiments carried out in his presence with a Leyden jar and by the contortions of courtiers receiving electric shocks. Benjamin Franklin's books, translated under the direction of M. de Buffon, were read as widely in the salons as those of Voltaire, Diderot and Rousseau.

Science was making industrial progress possible, and industrial progress was about to change the economic and social structure of Europe. The authors of the *Encyclopédie* were in fact among the Monarchy's most violent critics and the most implacable enemies of the Church. Their writings were colored by anticlericalism and hostility toward the Monarchy because they were

trying to explain to the masses the new discoveries —
not as scholars, which they definitely were not, but as
popularizers. That is to say, they were literary people
who did not understand that there was a possible com-
patibility between these new sciences and religion and
the established social order of the Monarchy. As a result of their enthusiasm for the sciences their work took
on a destructive character toward the other two factors.
Nevertheless it served a useful purpose, since the new
knowledge had to be popularized to get through to the
masses, who were naturally impatient to know the
meaning of the many fascinating new discoveries.

In history books for children, the first governments
of the French Republic made a point of emphasizing
the faults and vices of certain of the French kings —
referring, for instance, to the mistresses of Louis XV
rather than to the years of peace and prosperity that
the beginning of his reign had assured France. But
with less passion and a more objective point of view, it
must be admitted that Louis XV was an intelligent
ruler, a man of good will with a strong grasp of the
problems of his day. It is also to the great credit of the
Marquise de Pompadour that she played so well her
role of patroness of writers and artists. In fact, it seems
certain that, frivolous as she was, she was interested
in the lot of the common people. How could she have
been otherwise, surrounded as she was by her friends
the great economists, whose one ambition was to amel-

iorate the condition of the people? Moreover, if she had not thought as they thought, why would a sensitive philosopher like du Pont be moved to dedicate one of his works to her after her death? It was this much-denigrated court favorite who personally introduced Quesnay to the king. Louis XV heard out the great innovator's proposals with absorption and named him "*Le Penseur*"; the king personally designed Quesnay's coat-of-arms when he raised him to noble rank. Quesnay was also a member of the Encyclopedist group, and between 1750 and 1757 wrote for them a number of articles on agricultural subjects. Without actually withdrawing from their circle, he preferred, however, from time to time to publish his economic theories on his own responsibility, articles which he collected in a book called *Le Tableau Economique*. The king, who had been inspired by the theories of Rousseau to learn printing, had a special font of type cast for this publication. So, it was within the intimate presence of Louis XV and the Marquise de Pompadour that this profoundly original work was conceived.

It was an extraordinary thing that a young man like Pierre-Samuel Dupont, son of a watchmaker, should be admitted into the company of the powerful and celebrated of his period, to listen to what was being said and to take part in their discussions. Dupont owed this good fortune to Quesnay. This sponsorship was to be repaid, however, since it was Pierre-Samuel who invented the word "physiocracy" to denote the great man's economic system. A number of books have been devoted to Quesnay's original theories, which are based on the principle of "the natural order" and the idea that the "only real wealth" is what man takes from the soil by agriculture. Industry and commerce are only unproductive intermediaries in the distribution of this basic wealth. This being the case, it behooves a wise government to tax wealth at its source, namely landed property, but thereafter to let agricultural products circulate freely, and finally to do away with the innumerable taxes imposed, under a great variety of names, on agricultural products within the realm.

Since there is only one real form of wealth, the theory goes on to say, obviously a sensible government should favor those on whom it ultimately depends, that is, the farmers. In order for farming to prosper, it is evident that the ownership of land should be made available to the maximum possible number of people, and that the land should be cultivated in a scientific manner so as to obtain the greatest possible yield. To prevent a fall in prices through agricultural glut, is it not better to impose taxes on the "net product" (surplus after cost of production) and then let this net circulate freely? Thus the tax becomes a means of stabilizing the market.

"Property (which comes from a good government just as Natural Order comes from our Creator), security, and liberty — there is the social order." This was the creed of the physiocrats. And Quesnay added: "All men and all forms of power are subject to the Natural Order laid down by the Supreme Being; it is immutable and not to be denied." But how to apply these principles so as to develop the country's wealth? Nothing could be more simple. It was first necessary to make an exact inventory of national resources and Quesnay spent several years completing this task. It was in 1784 that the great chemist and philosopher, Lavoisier, who himself had never been a physiocrat, but who had read the writings of Quesnay and Dupont* with interest, published his own *Aperçu des Récoltes du Royaume*.

It is not possible in this narrative of the du Ponts to linger long on physiocracy. At this point it is expedient simply to state the reasonable hypothesis that physiocracy was at work in the minds of those who, with Jean-Jacques Rousseau, had just discovered in Nature a means of benefiting the class of people who alone produced "natural wealth." Later, all this was to arouse the indignation of socialists like Louis Blanc, who felt that the "people" no longer meant the peasants, but the industrial workers. However that may be, in progressive circles at the end of the reign of Louis XV, among those who were paving the way for the Revolution of 1789, physiocratic theory had a very great influence. Karl Marx recognized this fact. According to some, in Quesnay he admired the creator of the modern economy.

* For a partial list of Pierre-Samuel's writings see Bibliography.

Quesnay invented physiocracy, Pierre-Samuel Dupont gave it its name, and Turgot gave it a practical
form by using it as the groundwork for economic doctrines expressed in his *Traité sur la Formation et la Distribution des Richesses.* This work was written in 1766,
ten years before Adam Smith brought out his *Wealth
of Nations.* Turgot, who had applied his principles on
a local scale during his term of office as *Intendant* of
the province of Limousin, was soon to have an opportunity to put them to work on a national scale as Minister of Finance. Indeed, the young King Louis XVI
immediately upon accession to the throne in 1774 assigned him to this office. Turgot now called to his
support Pierre-Samuel Dupont, who had successfully
managed first the *Journal de l'Agriculture et du Commerce,* the physiocrats' organ, then the *Ephémérides
du Citoyen,* an economists' publication, before having
been named, in 1773, Councilor of the Margrave of
Baden at Karlsruhe. But Turgot was disappointed to
find that Dupont had gone to Poland to tutor the son
of a great Polish nobleman, Prince Czartoryski. Since
Pierre-Samuel had just married a young woman from the
little town of Nemours, near Fontainebleau, Mlle. Le
Dée de Rencourt, he had accepted the job because he
needed the money. But his self-exile would not last very
long, he had promised his friends. And, to prove this,
before leaving he had spent his first months' salary advance on the purchase of an estate called Bois des

Fossés, near the village of Chevannes and not far from Nemours. The property was sold to him by the Marquis de Mirabeau. For a friendly consideration, one may assume . . .

There is every reason to believe that when, in 1775 in distant Poland, Pierre-Samuel received Turgot's letter he did not hesitate about returning to France. He found reasons or excuses for turning over young Czartoryski to someone else's care and immediately on return was given the rather vague title of Inspector of Commerce. But he was, in fact, one of Turgot's closest collaborators. This explains why, when his "patron" suffered disgrace after the bloody riots of 1776 — events had proven that there was a big gap between physiocrat theory and practical application — Pierre-Samuel lost his post at the ministry. The free exchange of foreign produce had been disastrous, for the reason that industry in England was more efficiently organized than in France and English products were cheaper. Quesnay had died in 1774. Turgot, in turn, died in 1781. Meanwhile Pierre-Samuel had very philosophically retired to write a translation of *Orlando Furioso* and improve his estate at Chevannes. But he kept up his political contacts and was deeply interested in the cause of the American revolutionaries. Naturally, on a number of occasions — Chevannes is not far from Paris — he was in touch with Benjamin Franklin, Arthur Lee and Silas

Deane, the three American representatives sent by Congress to Versailles.

In October, 1781, after the defeat at Yorktown, the English realized they had lost the American colonies. It now became necessary to negotiate the peace. France, which had played such a big part in the Revolutionary War, was the most likely intermediary between Great Britain and America. Thus Vergennes, Minister of Foreign Affairs for Louis XVI since 1774, who was closely acquainted with Pierre-Samuel, knew that the American side would take kindly to his friend. He therefore charged him to confer with James Hutton, personal friend of Jefferson, who had just arrived in Paris. Between the two of them, they could get a rough draft of a peace treaty started. This document was not signed until 1783. It is recognized in history under the name of the Treaty of Paris. A plaque in the Rue Jacob, in the St. Germain des Prés quarter, marks the house where the signing took place. This treaty was actually the internationally legalized birth certificate of the Republic of the United States. The name of Pierre-Samuel does not figure in it for the reason that he was involved only in the preliminary draft, not in the definitive version. It is, true, nonetheless, that thereafter Pierre-Samuel Dupont's renown in America was greater than it ever had been in France, even though at home he had been made a member of seven learned academies and carried the titles of Councilor of the Margrave of Baden and Chevalier of the Order of Vasa. In 1785, for his work with the Americans, Louis XVI sent him a patent of nobility "for him and his posterity." *Le Grand Armorial de France* accords the Dupont coat-of-arms this description: "Quarters 1 and 4 of azure, with a gold column on a foreground of sinople; in 2 and 3, gules with gold chevrons." Above the shield is the motto "*Rectitudine sto.*" This patent granted him the privilege of being called Messire Dupont, a title about equal to "Sir" in England.*

In short, just four years before the Revolution, Dupont (on the patent of nobility the spelling is "Dupont," but shortly afterwards in this same period Pierre-Samuel began to sign his name "du Pont"†) became titled, and the physiocrat and watchmaker's son was an authentic aristocrat. Thus with no less authenticity his descendants are the same. It was not until sometime during the French Revolution that the du Ponts added "de Nemours," not, it can be said positively, to advertise to the new Sovereign People their membership in a class now so unpopular, but merely to distinguish themselves from all other Duponts now that Pierre-Samuel was

* One wonders why the American descendants of the Physiocrat have been using a coat of arms which does not correspond with the one listed in *Le Grand Armorial de France.* See illustration between pages 114 and 115.

† The du Ponts now write their name with a small *d,* but for clarity's sake in this book the capital is used in the name of the company.

so well known. For the name Dupont is as common in France as Smith in the United States.

The fact that an aristocratic connection does not always have the same validity must be borne in mind when closely examining current French titles. By ancient rule and tradition, a French title goes only to a direct male descendant. However, in modern times many families have ignored this and are today using titles as well as names which are in fact extinct. Such a one, well known to Americans, is Lafayette. The last male descendant of General de la Fayette died in 1890, according to Baron de Woelmar, erudite author of *Existing Nobility*. Also known to Americans is Rochambeau, the French nobleman who took part in the United States struggle for independence and whose relations still bear his title. It is interesting to note that the last Rochambeau — Philippe Auguste Donatien, the so-called "Marquis de Rochambeau" — also died without issue, in 1868.

Well known over the world is the laissez-faire attitude of the French Republic which permits anyone to call himself anything he thinks is proper to his situation, providing his pretension is not contested by other heirs.

In 1784 Pierre-Samuel was a handsome man of forty-six. Though not rich, he enjoyed a comfortable income. Owner of a pleasant estate, happily married and father of two children, one of whom had Turgot for godfather, the other the Marquis de Mirabeau, he was clearly held in high esteem by the leading personages of the realm. The future smiled at Pierre-Samuel in a new society where he was both accepted and well protected. But this society was made up of the tired people of a régime living in expectation of something, no one knew what, that would change things. In his *Survol de l'Histoire de France*, René Sédillot has aptly summed up the march of events during the period when du Pont received his aristocratic title: "The Industrial Revolution had been under way since Vaucanson, that mechanical magician, had invented a means of weaving by machine, and since the new sources of energy — oil, steam and gas — were beginning to give promise of great benefactions to mankind. The whole material aspect of life was changing fast but because of the king's failure to do his job, the monarchy bogged down in routine. . . ." And thus arrived the Revolution.

It was in the year before he was ennobled, on September 3, 1784, that the Physiocrat had the sorrow of losing his wife. He left Chevannes and came to take up residence in Paris with his sons, Victor, seventeen, and Eleuthère-Irénée, fourteen. In the apartment on Rue de la Corderie, these young people often had occasion to hear their father's friends discuss the topics of the day. Such conversation was bound to be instructive when these friends were Talleyrand, Lavoisier, Lafayette, Mme. de Staël, Franklin and Jefferson. Washington had named Thomas Jefferson minister plenipotentiary to Versailles in 1784. And so well did this American philosopher understand France that he became an expert in matters of French cuisine. The domestic servant by the name of James Hennings whom Jefferson brought with him from the United States shared his admiration for the "nice little dishes" of France, and he left no stone unturned to get the recipes. In Jefferson's library, which was to serve as the foundation of the Library of Congress, the cookbooks were catalogued under the general title of "Technical Arts." Grimod de la Reynière and Brillat-Savarin would certainly have approved such a classification. The friendship which developed between Jefferson and the Physiocrat was destined to play a major role in the American adventures of this French family.

July 14, 1789, the first day of the Revolution, was welcomed with rejoicing in the town houses of the Rue de la Corderie by the economists and philosophers who had for so long looked forward to it and who had done all they could to hasten its coming. On April 17, 1789, Pierre-Samuel had been elected deputy of the Third Estate to the Constituent Assembly from the district of Nemours. The Assembly was composed of elected representatives of the Nobles, the Clergy and the Common People. Members of the nobility, as du Pont and Honoré-Gabriel Mirabeau, sometimes chose to represent the

Third Estate. On July 14, when the Bastille was stormed, he was delighted, and he signed up for the National Militia along with his two sons. On August 4, when the Assembly of Nobles renounced all of their titled privileges, his enthusiasm was unbounded. And on the 27th — it goes without saying — he signed the Declaration of the Rights of Man.

In these days, it was necessary for a deputy to belong to a political club. In 1790 Pierre-Samuel joined the Club of '89, most prominent members of which were Sieyès, Monge, Bailly, André Chénier and Condorcet. This was considered a political error in the eyes of many because he was now labeled a moderate by his very membership in this club. From this action on, Pierre-Samuel du Pont ceased to be in the revolutionary movement. The ones who followed the wind had gone over to the extremist Jacobin Club. Perhaps Pierre-Samuel had nourished the illusion that it might be possible to steer the Revolution toward the physiocratic point of view. It was still two years before Louis XVI was dethroned on September 2, 1792.

When the Constituent Assembly was dissolving in 1791, it passed a law forbidding its members to sit in the new Legislative Assembly. His mandate thus having run out, Pierre-Samuel quit the scene. His older son, Victor, was in America serving as unpaid secretary of the French ambassador, the Comte de Moustiers. The younger son, Eleuthère-Irénée, was studying chemistry

at the National Powder Works under the tutelage of
Lavoisier, who since 1775 had been the head of the
State Administration of Powder (*Régie des Poudres*)
created by Turgot. Alone now, out of a job and with
little income, Pierre-Samuel declared: "If one loves lit-
erature, philosophy and public service, one must re-
tire into the publishing business." His deed was as good
as his word and, announcing that he was following in
the footsteps of Benjamin Franklin, he bought on l'Ile
St.-Louis, just across from Notre Dame Cathedral, a
printing establishment set up in the former Bretonvilliers town house. To sell his publications he also opened
a shop in the Rue de Richelieu. Though without much
work, he was actually very busy. The more time he had
on his hands, the more copiously he wrote, and he gave
over part of his presses to the printing of his own works.
As for the rest, there were orders from his old friends,
most of whom became his customers.

Among these customers, naturally, was Lavoisier,
whose *La Richesse Territoriale de la France* was in part
printed here. There was also in evidence now a Madame
Poivre, the agreeable widow of the colonial administra-
tor Pierre Poivre, who had died in 1786. To Poivre
France owes the spice culture of La Réunion (then
Bourbon) Island in the Indian Ocean. This intelligent
civil servant had succeeded in secretly transporting
spice plants taken by him from Dutch possessions in the
Pacific. At least two editions, dated Year II (that is,

after the Revolution), of his *Voyages d'un Philosophe* bear the imprint of Citizen du Pont's publishing house.

It was now that Eleuthère-Irénée, twenty years old, made a most romantic match. His wife, née Sophie Dalmas, was sixteen. Meanwhile, his teacher Lavoisier had quit the powder works at Essonnes to accept a Treasury post in Paris. He had been appointed *Fermier Général,* that is, one of the men in charge of financing the Monarchy. Lavoisier's move had brought Eleuthère-Irénée back to Paris near his father, and this was indeed lucky for Pierre-Samuel. Dreamer that he was, he had been taking poor care of his business, and his financial situation was becoming disturbing. He had had to mortgage his Chevannes property, Bois des Fossés, to get working capital for his printing house and he also had numerous unpaid bills and notes in arrears. Fortunately for the Physiocrat, Eleuthère-Irénée had found in his young Sophie a companion as practical as himself. Between the two of them they soon straightened out Pierre-Samuel's affairs.

The old Physiocrat, relieved of financial worry, fearlessly rushed toward other grave difficulties — this time arising from his independent political notions. However, it took more than rashness — it took disillusionment as well — to write such a pamphlet as the one I discovered recently in the La Rochelle Library, signed with the transparent pseudonym of Pontius Nemoracensis and published by "l'imprimerie Du Pont, Hôtel de Bretonvilliers." The pamphlet was not dated, but I believe it can be placed in 1792, around the time the king was dethroned.

Aristocracy is called [the pamphlet tells us] the arbitrary power exercised by a small number of men over a large number. . . . If, however, one turns from the consideration of ways used to banish liberty from empires to the observation of what goes on in . . . national assemblies, municipalities, sections, primary assemblies, electoral bodies, it will be seen that in spite of the support of reason and law, a numerous and virtuous majority, unhappily disunited and bereft of tactics, is nearly always forced to accede to a minority that would make you laugh if you knew how few, actually, its members were, but which is united, practiced, disciplined . . . and which knows how to throw stones of abuse and plunge home the dagger of calumny. . . . When a coalition of this present sort is formed, is it not just a new aristocracy? One which cares not a rap for the law and which lords it over the people? Turbulent minority, would that your aristocracy had held its tongue! The people wanted something else besides a change of tyrants.

On August 10, 1792, Pierre-Samuel damned himself irretrievably in the eyes of the rabid revolutionaries by joining the ranks of the Swiss Guards in their battle on the steps of the Tuileries in defense of the king. Sword in hand, Eleuthère-Irénée was beside his father. Many who, like Pierre-Samuel, had wept with joy at the storming of the Bastille were now outraged by the excesses of the *"purs."*

[33]

Among these was Delessert, Protestant banker, philosopher[*] and friend of progress, whose ideas approximated those of Mallet and Necker, eminent members of the so-called "Swiss group." Necker had made a fortune by timely speculation in English consolidated funds during the negotiations leading to the Treaty of Paris, an affair in which, as we have earlier noted, Pierre-Samuel had also taken part. After that Necker had financed the economists' movement largely responsible for the upheavals of '89. The historian Mathiez, speaking of these bankers, wrote: "The Court's defeat is understandable. . . . A government has its work cut out for it when Money is lined up against it." Louis Blanc, for his part, in his *Histoire de la Révolution,* claimed that the role of the Protestant publicists was just as important as that of the bankers. Be that as it may, in 1792 the Protestant Delesserts and the Protestant du Ponts had much the same reaction. Etienne Delessert, who with his father had assisted in the storming of the Bastille, had also rushed to the aid of the Swiss Guards in '92. Denounced by the patriots after this courageous act, Etienne had saved his life by emigrating to America, where he founded a bank and bought extensive properties before dying of yellow fever in 1796 at the age of thirty-three.

[*] In 1792 Delessert (1735-1816) had founded the first fire insurance company and the first bank of discount. His son, Benjamin (1773-1847) in Paris set up the first cotton spinning mill in France, and later, the first mill for the manufacture of sugar from sugar beets.

The du Ponts, however, at first did not dream of leaving France. But a price had been put on Pierre-Samuel's head, and his sons — Victor having come back shortly before from America — undertook to hide him. Haste was of the essence. Howling mobs had sacked his apartment and vandalized the printing house. Pierre-Samuel was saved in the nick of time by being lodged in a hideaway that the scholarly Lalande had set up for his use in the cupola of the Institute. There every day a pupil of Lalande, the young Harmand, was furnishing him with food and fresh news. It was not until September 2 that Pierre-Samuel, spirited out of the building in disguise by Harmand, successfully made a getaway from Paris to go into hiding at Cormeille-en-Parisis, where he was passed off as a doctor. There he played his part very well, probably killing or curing his patients no more, no less, than his medical colleagues.

The tumult having finally died down for an interval, Pierre-Samuel made his way back to Bois des Fossés, where Sophie, his daughter-in-law, had been successfully in charge during his absence. Having time on his hands, he went to work on what he hoped would be his major literary work, an opus to be entitled *La Philosophie de l'Univers*. He wrote this in the form of intimate letters to his close friends, the Lavoisiers, husband and wife. Restless, Pierre-Samuel had begun to show himself again. Did he believe he was out of danger because his older son, Victor, had just been given a *"brevet de*

Civisme" by the commune of Chevannes, and on top of that had been promoted to *"gendarme,"* that is, member of the security troops at headquarters for the canton of Ferrière? Despite this, the fact remains that on June 20, 1794, a squad of patriots came to his home to arrest him and take him to La Force prison, formerly the Paris mansion of the Duke de la Force.

A month earlier Lavoisier had been guillotined. The honest Lavoisier had been accused, along with the other *Fermiers Généraux,* of stealing from the people. This job was notorious for its graft-amassing possibilities. The revolutionaries judged Lavoisier by the others, forgetting that he was already rich and had spent his personal fortune in search of scientific knowledge to benefit mankind. The infamous remark on that day was *"La République n'a pas besoin de savants"* — no need for scientists! Pierre-Samuel had no doubt in his mind that the same fate awaited him. And so it was that during this imprisonment he wrote his *Memoirs,* to leave to posterity testimony of his experiences.

At the same time he wrote a great many letters. In the most fateful of these, he notes that "poor Alexandre de Beauharnais [fickle husband of the Josephine who was to marry Bonaparte] had the misfortune to arrive [at La Force] on the first of July, 1794, and was beheaded"; he adds that it was his own good luck that the mail was late, so that the order for his own execution — scheduled for July 25 — did not arrive until after July 27 (10 Thermidor), the day the Terror ended.

Thus is was a whimsy of fate that du Pont escaped the massacres. Upon his release from La Force, he returned to Bois-des-Fossés. In the country his daily existence was certainly easier than in the capital, where no food supplies were coming in and black market commodities were commanding fabulous prices. A short while later he was elected a member of the Academy of Moral and Political Sciences. The following year the Canton of Nemours sent him as representative to the Council of Ancients. The same year — 1795 — he founded a journal called *L'Historien*. Almost immediately, he fearlessly put aside the lessons of the past. He used *L'Historien* to attack the government of the Directoire. And on 18 Fructidor in the Year IV (September 4, 1797) Pierre-Samuel was again under prosecution. This time the guillotine was not being used; instead some 163 "enemies of the Republic," 17 of them deputies, were deported to Cayenne in Guiana, a fate almost worse. But for the intervention of Marie-Joseph Chénier and a sympathetic word from Tallien, Pierre-Samuel very probably would have been deported, since Barras did not like him. Chénier evoked compassion among the Physiocrat's accusers — Mme. de Staël's clever idea — by pretending that du Pont was an octogenarian. Bald and bent, Pierre-Samuel looked far older than his age. However, at the time he was not more than fifty-eight, and he must have still been relatively hale, since two years earlier he had married M. Poivre's widow!

After this new hairbreadth escape Pierre-Samuel began making preparations to go to America. His wife, who was not afraid of long sea voyages, urged him on. His son Victor, who had come back to France, as we have seen, in the very midst of the Revolution, again left, after the Terror, to serve as consul in Charleston. It was from Rochefort, very near La Rochelle, that Victor embarked in 1795 for the United States aboard the frigate *La Méduse*. This was the same vessel — wrecked in 1816 — which the painter Géricault immortalized in a gigantic composition now in the Louvre.

Victor's voyage passed without incident, and he landed at Newport, Rhode Island, in June. After a stay in Philadelphia, then the national capital, he left for Charleston and there took up his post as French consul. He and his wife liked it there very much and were not at all enthusiastic about having to leave in 1798, when Talleyrand promoted him to consul-general in Philadelphia. He arrived at the capital to discover that the President, John Adams, a firm supporter of the Jay Treaty and above all desirous of re-establishing commercial relations with England, refused to receive him, under the pretext that privateers of the French Republic had seized American ships which in principle were neutral. Unable under the circumstances to present his credentials, and finding himself unwittingly mixed up in a quarrel between his native land and this America which he had begun to love, Victor nonetheless succeeded in getting an interview with President Adams on a purely private basis. This interview served only to show him that the President detested Pierre-Samuel. According to Victor's diary, Adams reproached the old Physiocrat for being, all at once, "too philosophical, too moderate . . . and too jacobin"! This eminent statesman was not, as a matter of fact, so far off the mark as it might seem at first blush.

Victor did not achieve accreditation. Unable to occupy the position assigned to him by his government, he returned to France with his wife and children. As soon as he got to Paris, he wasted no time briefing Talleyrand on what had happened. It was after hearing this report that Talleyrand resolved to do something to relieve relations between the two republics. What then ensued is embedded in Victor's letter at the beginning of this book. Victor's trip to La Rochelle, where he wrote that letter, had not been immediately decided upon by Talleyrand. It had been preceded by persuasive negotiations between Paris and Philadelphia which had induced President Adams to send an ambassador to Paris, without bothering to ask the advice of Congress. Eight years later, about to die, this President who had been

so incensed against the French asked that the following
be inscribed on his tomb:

HERE LIES JOHN ADAMS, WHO TOOK TO HIMSELF
THE RESPONSIBILITY OF PEACE WITH FRANCE . . .

It is never easy to understand history, but quite impossible to understand it by reading epitaphs on burial
monuments.

Through Victor, Pierre-Samuel knew how things
stood in regard to American feeling toward his compatriots, but he also knew that his plans were a "special
case" and that he could count on the support of his
faithful friends Vice-President Jefferson, James Hutton
and Benjamin Franklin. This was probably why he
turned down Victor's suggestion that he wait a few
months before getting under way. He had roughed out
his plan of colonization in Virginia. This was not such
an original project, coming after the plan of Bernardin
de Saint-Pierre (philosopher and author of the famous
romantic novel *Paul et Virginie*), who had hoped to
found an agricultural colony in Russia. Like Saint-
Pierre's plan, never achieved, it was inspired by the
philosophical ideals of that era — the return to nature,
mother-earth, and so forth. These were the dreams to
which Frenchmen clung all the more tenaciously now
that the value of money was dropping swiftly and stead-

ily and the government was so corrupt that the worst could be confidently expected.

Pierre-Samuel's rough plan of colonization in Virginia was composed of two parts. First, there would be a du Pont de Nemours office in Alexandria, Virginia, chosen no doubt for the prestige of being near the cradle of many of the great men who had founded the Republic, and also because it was near Washington, where they were talking of relocating the capital. Furthermore, Alexandria was not far from the land that they aspired to buy and exploit in the James River Valley — a matter of nearly a million acres. Second, there would be a du Pont de Nemours office in New York, America's largest port. With Alexandria charged with agricultural affairs, New York was obviously the right place to centralize banking and European import operations.

All this provided a continuing pretext for the indefatigable Pierre-Samuel to resume his activities as a publicist overflowing with ideas, a publisher overloaded with work. Plunging into the composition of maps and estimates, he personally wrote out and printed the alluring prospectus expounding to future subscribers the idea of the two companies and the profits to be derived from capital entrusted to him for the great American venture. There would be farmland of incredible fertility on which model villages would be built, provided, it went without saying, with all the necessary industrial complement — sawmills, potteries, gristmills, distilleries, and so on, not forgetting schools, hospitals, inns and churches. How much would it take for all this? A trifling four million francs.

At 10,000 francs a share, Pierre-Samuel would be able to raise among his friends, he believed, a total subscription of 3,200,000 francs. But the truth of the matter was that all they had come up with so far was promises.

No longer in the French diplomatic service, Victor had been dispatched — as we have already learned from his letter from La Rochelle — to the West of France. Meanwhile, Pierre-Samuel, accompanied by his wife, had gone to ring doorbells in Holland. As for Eleuthère-Irénée, he had stayed on in Paris, since he had been entrusted with the dual mission of informing himself on agricultural questions at the Jardin des Plantes and of selling the printing house on the Ile St.-Louis at the highest possible price. There was only one paid subscription, that of the Swiss banker Bidermann. In pledge of his shares he had handed over the title of a property of 6000 French acres (each equivalent to 1¼ English acres) in the state of Kentucky. In principle, 214 shares had been subscribed by Necker, Mme. de Staël's uncle, by Beaumarchais, Lafayette, La Tour-Maubourg, and others. But so far, no money.

Getting impatient, Pierre-Samuel named Bureaux de Pusy, his second wife's son-in-law, to be director of the

New York office.* Bureaux de Pusy was a military engineer by profession and had been one of Lafayette's
companions during the American Revolution. In May,
1799, he was sent on ahead with the ex-Mme. Poivre,
now Pierre-Samuel's wife, on a vessel sailing from Le
Havre, to feel out the situation overseas. After a vexa-
tious incident — an English cruiser stopped the vessel
for inspection and Bureaux de Pusy was detained for
three months in London — he arrived in New York in
August. There an alarming letter from France soon
caught up with him. The subscribers had not lived up
to their promises. There was only 450,000 francs in the
cash box. At the same time — another blow — the bank
set up in Paris by Pierre-Samuel to serve as correspond-
ent for the one planned for the United States had already gone bankrupt! Had this troublesome beginning
discouraged Pierre-Samuel? Not at all! He announced
that the departure on the *American Eagle* from La
Rochelle as arranged by Victor would take place the
minute the vessel was shipshape. Skeptical at first, Victor soon became as enthusiastic as his father. Even the
prudent Eleuthère-Irénée let himself be carried away
by his father's optimism.

* Victor had hoped to marry Julie-Isle-de-France Poivre, but she
had preferred Bureaux de Pusy. This detail will perhaps clarify incidents coming up later in this recital.

2

Good Connections

As SOON AS HE had arrived in New York, Bureaux
de Pusy had looked around for a house near the
city where the whole family could live, at least for the
time being. His choice had fallen on a property which
he was able to pick up at a good price, located some
ten miles from New York near Bergen Point, New Jersey. Early in January, 1800, Pierre-Samuel and his clan
were reunited there, excited and happy after their
dreadful three months on the ocean. The house that
had been called Good Stay became Gallicized into Bon
Séjour.

From Bon Séjour Pierre-Samuel wrote to Vice-President Thomas Jefferson to let him know he was in the
United States. No doubt Jefferson was already aware of

his friend's projects, because Bureaux de Pusy had forwarded a letter from him to his father-in-law which had been waiting for him several days when he arrived at his new home. It was addressed to Mr. Dupont the Elder, Bergen Point, Near New York (New Jersey). In this letter Jefferson warmly welcomed the du Pont family. It was written in English, a language Pierre-Samuel could neither speak nor write and barely understood. Despite his efforts he never succeeded in learning English, and the long correspondence between the two men has the peculiarity of being written in two different tongues. This correspondence was published in America in 1931 by Professor Chinard. A passage from Pierre-Samuel's very first letter to Thomas Jefferson, written in France before he and his family had sailed from La Rochelle, is especially noteworthy:

I will describe my situation for you in detail, my desires, obligations and means. . . . One of our advantages is the fact that there are four men among us, Pusy, my two sons and myself, none of whom is lacking in intelligence and goodness, and by a near miracle each of us has a wife filled with good sense, judgment, courage and a desire to make out well. A *quaternion* like this, four such perfectly assorted households, and eight persons of such talent, so virtuous and so intimately united, is something I have yet to see except in this instance. And we have you to keep us from making mistakes. Whoever is Almighty, may He bless you for it. . . .*

* *"Qui que ce soit en soit béni."*

Reading this, Corneille's phrase comes to mind — "I know what I am worth. . . ." Nevertheless, though Pierre-Samuel might be short on modesty, it is likely he was not so far from the truth when he played up the fact that not often did a family group like his come to put down roots in American soil. At the beginning of the nineteenth century most immigrants came from a have-not background. For the most part manual laborers drawn from countries with a large surplus population, they were, to be sure, useful to an America short on manpower, but several generations would have to pass before these needy immigrants were educated, civilized and technically trained. With the du Pont de Nemours this problem did not exist.

Capital was very scarce in America. Little of it was coming in from Europe, and especially little from France, where not much was left after the Revolution. Only a few Dutch investors had bought large tracts of land for development purposes in response to a prospectus which was widely circulated in Amsterdam in 1792, for the Holland Land Company. This pamphlet was entitled *Ideas Offered to the Capitalists of Europe on the Immense Benefits to Be Gained from Buying Uncultivated Land in the United States of America*. The du Ponts of course had seen this and, as events proved, were among those impressed.

There had been much talk in France, often highly exaggerated, about the successes of the Holland Land

[46]

Company. The letter to Jefferson was written as a result of the idea Pierre-Samuel had of launching such a company himself, since the du Ponts had been greatly interested and impressed by what Victor's friend Robert Fulton had told them. According to Fulton, splendid land could be purchased in Kentucky for twelve francs an acre.

This was an unusual family of new colonists who were greeted upon their arrival by Vice-President Jefferson. They were businessmen who would contribute, as Jefferson must have viewed it, to the wealth of the country through the movements of international exchange they would soon create.

It might be worthwhile to underscore the curious formula used by Pierre-Samuel at the end of his letter to Jefferson: *"Qui que ce soit en soit béni!"* We must not leave the impression that this phrase was of such nature as to shock a man like Jefferson, whose religious ideas were basically as vague as those of the Physiocrat who had been so impressed by Rousseau. The instigators of the American Revolution certainly did not hold to the same views as the early settling Puritans. Franklin put Socrates and Jesus on the same footing, like the Unitarians who in 1959 discussed long and hard before signing a declaration recognizing the divinity of Christ. Gouverneur Morris was as much of an atheist as Voltaire, and Ethan Allen, hero of Ticonderoga, got along nicely with the cult of the Goddess of Reason.

To get an idea of Pierre-Samuel's personal religion, we must go back to the following passage from a letter he had written in other years to Lavoisier: "I am a maker of clocks myself, with whatever little I may have of spirit. The immense clock of the Universe also has a clockmaker. . . . Who is he? About this matter I know nothing. . . ." In 1947 one of his descendants discovered in the Library of Congress a copy of a little volume dedicated by Pierre-Samuel* to Jefferson and entitled: *On the Religion of His Fathers and Our Fathers (Sur la Religion de Ses Pères et de Nos Pères)*. The book was printed in Paris in 1808. From this work it is evident that fifteen years after having written the above letter to Jefferson, the Physiocrat had not changed his religious views. He dumped all religions, one may say, into one basket, and saw their ministers as nothing more than "useful magistrates of morality." No more than that.

The influence of Freemasonry was as obvious in the writings of Pierre-Samuel du Pont as it was in the works of other French philosophers; and this same influence had spread rapidly over the New World. As early as 1721 the lodges founded in Canada had begun to branch out into the English colonies in what was to become the United States. By 1734 there were several lodges in Virginia, Pennsylvania, New Jersey and Mas-

* In this volume Pierre-Samuel used the pseudonym Irénée Bonfils.

sachusetts. The Grand Master of American Masonry (of the Scottish Rite) was Joseph Warren. Washington, Jefferson, Franklin, were all Masons, as in France were the majority of the leaders of the French "progressive" movement, such as Voltaire, Lavoisier, Lalande, Quesnay, Lafayette, Necker, the Duke of Orleans, the Princess of Lamballe, and the Duchess of Choiseul. And so was Pierre-Samuel.

Just four days after the death of his first wife, Nicole, a revealing ceremony had been staged by the Physiocrat for his son Eleuthère-Irénée, which he described in this manner: "I waited for him in a high-backed chair, sword at my side, ribbon across my coat, a cushion at my feet, a bust of his mother at my left, and the young man's sword and hat to the right on a bench, etc. . . ." There is a modern painting by Stanley Arthurs in the Hagley Museum in Wilmington (see illustration) which depicts this curiously pompous event in which the father was obviously imbued with the Masonic spirit. Pierre-Samuel profited by this occasion to give his children some good advice. "No privilege exists that is not essentially bound to an obligation. The Nation confers the right to bear arms on families judged to be most distinguished by way of education, . . . by virtue of a more delicate sense of honor, a stronger sense of probity, a dominant inclination to use all their strength and to sacrifice their life for the public good." After Pierre-Samuel had saluted his two sons with his sword and kissed them, he said: "Promise, both of you, always to stand together, to assuage each other's pain, to help each other in all your work, to succor each other no matter what the risk or danger. . . . May Heaven bless your labors and your posterity. May each generation of your descendants ceaselessly apply themselves to the betterment of that which in time they will leave behind. . . ."

It was unquestionably through being a Mason that Pierre-Samuel got to know Talleyrand. The historian Lacour-Gayet discovered that Talleyrand, the future Bishop of Autun, "was the first master of the lodge that he had established in 1786 together with the Duke of Orleans . . . and out of which was to grow . . . the first version of the Jacobin Club." Lacour-Gayet also found proof that Pierre-Samuel du Pont was one of the members of the mysterious Society of the Thirty, in the roster of which "the name of Le Pelletier de Saint-Fargeau, La Rochefoucauld, d'Aiguillon, Condorcet, Sieyès, La Fayette and Talleyrand were also found." Members of this society were "recruited from two of the most exclusive lodges of the Grand Orient, the lodge of the Nine Sisters, which was frequented by the *philosophes*, and the lodge of Rue du Coq-Héron, frequented by the *grands seigneurs*. . . . It has been supposed, reasonably enough, that to belong to the Society of the Thirty one had to have risen to the Masonic rank of Chevalier Kaddoch or the 30th Degree. . . ." If

Lacour-Gayet's supposition is correct, the Physiocrat Pierre-Samuel was not only a Mason, but a high dignitary of the Freemasonry movement.

I have found no evidence that Eleuthère-Irénée was ever a member of a lodge. (His mother being a devout Roman Catholic, he had made his First Communion and thus might have preferred not to be affiliated with Masonry.*) On the other hand, I found in New York an almost forgotten document showing that Victor was one of the founders, in 1801, of a New York lodge called *La Sincérité*, which is still in existence. Now as then, it is mainly composed of Frenchmen, or the descendants of French families. It is not known when or where Victor was initiated, but it was probably at the beginning of his diplomatic career. In January, 1808, he signed a petition seeking the installation of a lodge at Angelica, New York. In 1813 he was received into the Washington Lodge No. 1 at Wilmington, Delaware. From 1822 to 1826 he was Grand Marshal of the Franklin Lodge in the same city. It was under this title, moreover, that he was charged with organizing a special reception to honor Lafayette, who had returned to the United States to dedicate on October 6, 1824, amid great pomp and ceremony, a monument to Joseph Warren, Grand Master of American Masonry (of the Scottish rite), who was killed at the battle of Bunker Hill.

---

* Pope Clement XII in his bull *In eminenti* (April 25, 1738) had forbidden Catholics to become Freemasons.

Back in December 27, 1769, well before the du Ponts had settled in Delaware, a charter was granted to Lodge No. 13 at Christiana Ferry, afterward Wilmington. Before this time, it appears that Masons in this territory were affiliated with the Royal Arch branch of Masonry introduced in 1758 in Philadelphia, which was, according to William R. Singleton and A. Gallatin Mackey, authors of the *History of Freemasonry*, the seat of the first authentic branch in the North American English colonies. In any case, many leading members of the lodge were immigrants from France and the French colony of Santo Domingo. The hostility of the local Quakers to the strange secret doings of these foreigners probably explains their terrified reactions to a curious incident occurring in the same year, 1758. A certain Dr. Cappelle of Philadelphia, former surgeon of the French army, had died in Wilmington, and members of his lodge decided to bury him according to Masonic funeral rites. It was during the summer, the sky cloudless. Suddenly, right in the middle of the ceremony, there was a cyclonic whirlwind and the sky went black as night. The Quaker population was certain that this manifestation of heaven's wrath was proof that Freemasonry was linked with the powers of hell.

It might be said that because Pierre-Samuel and Victor were Masons and because they were Protestants, they gained many advantages in America. But on the other hand, while Pierre-Samuel was in the campaign-planning stage of his American business debut these considerations were not enough to exempt them entirely from certain difficulties. The blunders of the French Directoire had not yet been forgotten, nor were the stupidities of Citizen Genêt, sent in 1793 as first minister of the new French Republic to Philadelphia. Public opinion was still aroused over those captured ships. Victor had been right in advising his father to postpone departure for America a few months. And Jefferson, as is known from his letters, shared this opinion. Pierre-Samuel understood all this now, too late.

Considering this mood, it is doubtful whether the Americans paid much attention to the prose of Pierre-Samuel's circulars. "The head of our house," these circulars announced, "is du Pont de Nemours. Suffice it to say that he is known as the pupil and very intimate friend of the illustrious Turgot. . . . He has come to live in America in consequence of persecutions suffered by . . . the friends of Justice, Order, Peace, Morality and true Liberty. . . . Our second director is Bureaux de Pusy . . . who, having shared the misfortunes and imprisonment of La Fayette, had his rights as French Citizen restored the same time as he . . ."

The circular, printed in France, concluded with these words: "Besides our house in New York, we hope soon to establish another in Alexandria, Virginia."

The realities encountered on American territory were

soon to rid Pierre-Samuel of some of his illusions. First, he discovered that the joint stock company arrangement he had chosen for his company as the most practical formula was not legally valid in American eyes. He then learned that in the great majority of the states, including New Jersey, it was impossible to obtain naturalization papers without at least five years' residence, and that foreigners, moreover, were prohibited from buying land. Finally — and this thwarted the anticipated formation of an export-import company — he found that the American government not only was imposing a very high excise tax on imports of foreign manufactured goods, but on top of that was exacting a surtax on goods sold abroad by foreign middlemen, thus making export likewise difficult.

The winter was cold at Bon Séjour, and their house "on the arm of the sea that separates the island of New York from the mainland on the New Jersey side, exactly opposite Staten Island," was much too small to accommodate a family of fourteen without regular employment. There was also the problem that some means of getting around the law had to be found if the original plan were to be carried out — either that, or change the plan. Spring arrived, and still nothing had turned up. The head of the family, optimistic as ever, spent his days writing. He had been elected member of yet another academy, this time the American Philosophical Society, and he was composing a treatise on public education, vaguely commissioned by Jefferson. Since it was important that at least one of the du Ponts become a citizen as soon as possible, Victor left for Virginia. In Virginia, foreigners were not prohibited from buying property, and being a property-owner automatically made one a citizen of this state. With this in mind, Victor bought a tract of land in the vicinity of Alexandria, then went with his wife and two children to take up residence in a house on Pearl Street in New York. The young household's New York quarters would serve the company both as social seat and banking establishment. In May, Victor rented something better at 91 Liberty Street. Pierre-Samuel went along with this change, the new house being much more attractive and equipped to give future customers a more favorable impression. The customers still remained in the future, but this did not prevent Pierre-Samuel's facile imagination from working at top pressure. He had already mapped out a number of projects capable of earning large revenues, such as a rapid courier service between America and Europe, the revitalizing of Guadeloupe, a liaison between Mexico and Spain. . . . But his two sons — and very likely their wives even more — began to chafe in their idleness; for the money was melting away, and the family might soon be without resources.

In the fall of 1800, an incident occurred which had long-lasting consequences for all the du Ponts. Mme.

Victor du Pont relates in her *Souvenirs* that a friend of Victor's, Colonel Toussard (in a memoir of the period his name appears as de Tousard), "while talking about this and that, mentioned a little establishment in Pennsylvania where gunpowder was manufactured. Irénée, who had studied this sort of thing during his youth, declared his intention of visiting this manufacturer. The plan was carried out and he was extremely surprised to see that those in charge were making powder by methods dating from the reign of Louis XIV, and were completely ignorant of the progress two centuries had brought to this industry. These manufacturers, however, were doing an excellent business. . . ." This is how Mme. Victor du Pont explains the initial idea of making gunpowder. But perhaps the other, more romantic, version — the one officially accredited by the Du Pont Company and apparently part of the "family tradition" — may be preferred:

"One day, Irénée, who had been introduced to the Colonel by Victor, went on a hunting party with him. A retired artillery officer, Toussard lived near Wilmington in the state of Delaware. He extolled the advantages one had as a Frenchman in this town because of the fact that a little French colony, composed in part of people escaped from Santo Domingo, had settled there. That afternoon, the hunters having used up their powder, Toussard went looking for some in a village store. Irénée noted that he insisted on powder with an English trademark. Much surprised, he asked the Colonel why he did not buy American powder instead. 'Because,' the other told him, 'they don't have any of it here that isn't expensive and at the same time very bad.' Having learned this, Irénée returned home greatly excited and did not sleep a wink that night. The next day he let his father know about his great project: The du Ponts would become powder-makers in America. They would either buy an existing mill and modernize it, or would build one themselves. . . ."

Take your choice of the two versions. To accept the second, it remains to be imagined how the Colonel could go hunting in 1800 — since he had lost an arm fighting alongside Lafayette in the American Revolution. . . . But let us not tamper with legend. What is certain is that Eleuthère-Irénée, perhaps because he was the Physiocrat's "sensible son," or perhaps simply because he was thirty years old, with a wife and two children to look out for, was no dreamer of dreams. Nor was he, like Brillat-Savarin — the famous gourmet — the kind of man who saw no more in a hunting party during his American exile than a chance to kill a wild turkey and regale himself with it because it was "charming to look at, gratifying to smell and delicious to taste . . ." (*Physiologie du Goût*).

But as a sequel to either story — and here history and tradition are in harmony — Eleuthère-Irénée, accompanied by the Colonel, visited at least one powder

[57]

works and perhaps two. This was enough to convince him of the incredible ignorance of the American managers.

Then, having carefully made his estimates — like any good student of Lavoisier who knew his business — he arrived at the conclusion that $30,000 would be enough capital to set up and operate for a year a powder mill with an annual productive capacity of 160,000 pounds. The rough outline of his plan has been recovered and religiously preserved:

120,000 lbs. saltpeter @ 10¢	$12,000.00
20,000 lbs. sulphur @ 2¢	400.00
20,000 lbs. charcoal @ 1¢	200.00
1 overseer	638.75
4 foremen	2,190.00
12 laborers	6,397.50
Manager's salary	2,000.00
Miscellaneous, wastage, etc.	4,183.75
Machinery repairs	2,000.00

Since the sale of 160,000 pounds of powder at prevailing American prices would bring in $40,000, the net gain would be $10,000 a year. Presented in this fashion, we may suppose, the project was not of a nature to evoke the enthusiasm of Pierre-Samuel, used as he was to dealing — in his imagination — with millions. But the rest of the family reacted so favorably that he pronounced himself ready to endorse his younger son's idea. On December 17, 1800, after not quite a year in America, he wrote to Jefferson:

When my children, whom I am sending to Europe on business for us, have returned, I am going to settle in Alexandria, where I have purchased a house in order to have the enjoyment of your good works within closer reach. . . . One of my sons, whom Lavoisier instructed for five years in the manufacture [of powder] for the Gun Powder Administration and who is one of the best powder-makers in France, where the best powders in the world are made, will set up here a fine manufactory for this material [so] indispensable to the defense of the States. The purpose of his trip to France is to bring back copper and bronze machines which we cannot have made here as fast or as well for triple the cost. . . . I dare to allege that he will make bullets that go a fifth or more greater distance than English or Dutch bullets. And in light of this promise, I beg you not to let out any contract for supplying your powder magazines before you have compared what we are making with others. . . .

What we are making? Indeed, he was ahead of himself, to say the least! But Pierre-Samuel, as we are beginning to realize, lived outside the limits of the real. By way of postscript he added this eulogy of his friend, who had just been elected President: "I believe that Europe, the Sciences, Philosophy and Morality should share in these congratulations. My sons send you their respects. It is my desire that the oldest, who has two children born in South Carolina, and who has taken the oath of allegiance in Virginia, should be completely naturalized as soon as possible."

Reading these extracts from the letter, one is constrained to ask himself whether the invention of the art of "public relations," hitherto attributed to Americans, did not in fact arise with the Frenchman Pierre-Samuel du Pont de Nemours. Victor was quickly naturalized at Dunfries. A convinced pacifist, Jefferson could not help being delighted to see the birth of an industry so useful in the defense of his country. He replied in this vein to Victor's father and Irénée. Both the sons, meanwhile, had just set sail for France, charged with carrying out a very explicit mission: To bring back machinery, money and, if possible, technicians to help Eleuthère-Irénée set up his powder works in the United States.

3

Two Brothers, or the Perfect Union

> Our happiness depends on living virtuously and close to nature.
>
> BERNARDIN DE SAINT-PIERRE
> *Paul et Virginie*

AT THE END OF JANUARY, 1801, a little more than a year after their arrival in Newport, the du Pont brothers were on their way back to France. The roles they would assume had been divided up in advance: Victor, the diplomat, would make use of his connections to line up whoever might be needed; Eleuthère-Irénée, the chemist, would step to the fore whenever technical questions arose.

The Paris to which the two young men returned only remotely resembled the one they had left. Dread of troubled tomorrows no longer existed now that the Directoire had been replaced by the Consular régime. Parisians who had earlier taken to the provinces as a precautionary measure had returned in great numbers

to the capital. But more than this, Paris had again become the universal pole of attraction that it was in the
good old days of the eighteenth century. In February,
1801, Paris was so crowded that the du Ponts had
trouble even finding cramped quarters at the Hôtel des
Etrangers. And it was not until several days later that
they were able to find more suitable lodgings at the
Hôtel de Paris, Rue de Richelieu. We have firsthand
information about their voyage across and their Paris
stay, thanks to the diary which Victor kept in English.
Through this diary we can get a good idea of the number of influential people the brothers knew and what
their father's renown in France was worth to du Pont
business affairs. On February 16, Victor was received
by Consul Lebrun. Invited to dine at the Tuileries,
where this high dignitary was living in Marie Antoi-
nette's old apartments, he was struck by the change evident there. "It is surprising," he records in his notebook,
"to see how every man has turned courtier since there
is a Court, for the present government is the first since
the Revolution which has affected to copy the Ancien
Régime, its politeness, its splendor, its dignity. . . ."
On February 17, at Château de Neuilly, the showplace
which Talleyrand, the minister of foreign affairs, had
reserved for his own enjoyment, and which was later to
be occupied by King Louis-Philippe, a huge reception
was staged in honor of the First Consul, Bonaparte, on
the occasion of the signing of the Treaty of Lunéville.

Having been asked to attend, Victor had a chance to see at close range nearly all the outstanding personalities of the period. And he was Parisian enough to recount in his diary the gossip that was making the rounds.

One of the main attractions of the soirée, he tells us, was an Italian artiste, Grassini, "a very handsome woman," whose diamonds were as famous as her voice. "It is reported that Bonaparte gave her part of these diamonds in Italy and I remarked that he seemed very pleased during her singing and Mme. Bonaparte quite out of humor, for she is very jealous of him. . . ." During the reception Victor had an opportunity to meet an old friend of his father's again: "It was this evening that I saw La Fayette for the first time since June, 1791. . . . I had a fair view of Bonaparte, having General La Fayette on my arm when he stopped to ask him how he was and if he had news from his son. (Washington La Fayette has been severely wounded at a late affair in Italy under General Rochambeau) . . . La Fayette has grown fat; he wears a brown wig and it makes in him the greatest alteration. . . ." On February 21 he dined at the ever-busy Mme. de Staël's, "where one finds a curious mixture of men of all parties." On the 25th Victor ran into an American friend, George Waddell of Philadelphia, and then had tea at Mme. Lavoisier's, where with emotion he heard memories of the past evoked. Evidently this widowed lady had not yet chosen her second husband. He was to be Benjamin Thompson, an American with an extraordinary career. Born at Woburn, Massachusetts, in 1753, knighted by King George III, and later, in Bavaria, Minister of War and Police and the Grand Chamberlain of the Elector, Mr. Thompson played a big role under his title of Count Rumford. Unhappily for Mme. Lavoisier, this marriage ended in divorce.

One difficult thing about succeeding in business is not so much having something of interest to propose as finding someone to propose it to. But without extending himself, Victor had all the contacts he needed. And he knew how to make the most of them.

Victor's first success, undoubtedly gained through the intercession of Josephine, whom he had known in earlier years — she, too, was a Freemason initiated at Strasbourg — was to get an appointment with Robin, commissar of the Gunpowder Administration. Under Fouché, former member, now defrocked, of the Fathers of the Oratory, Bonaparte's police were well informed, and it is likely that he had been kept in touch with the du Pont mission and had given instructions to Commissar Robin, one of his top-ranking officials. And it was quite natural that Bonaparte should look with favor on the establishment in America of a mill that would be harmful to British exports. Eleuthère-Irénée's conference with Robin had an unexpected outcome. It was agreed that the Essonnes engineers would design the powder mill, that they would let Eleuthère-Irénée in on their trade secrets and that the State would sell him, at cost, machinery to be taken back to the United States. This much accomplished, the question of financing the enterprise ceased to be a problem.

Six months later Eleuthère-Irénée returned to America. Victor, for his part, decided to stay on a little while in France and Spain, believing that with the business climate now more favorable he could find the backing that the du Ponts had unsuccessfully tried to get for their New York firm before they left La Rochelle on the *Eagle*. This undertaking had never been abandoned. Nor had the du Ponts entirely given up their agricultural projects. Indeed, it was on their account that Eleuthère-Irénée had been commissioned to bring back from France, along with his packing cases of machinery, some purebred Merino sheep to serve as the basis for a large-scale breeding operation in America. For a variety of reasons Eleuthère-Irénée was unable to take the animals along on his ship when he embarked, but they did arrive on a later ship.

Taking advantage of all the spare time at his disposal during the crossing, Eleuthère-Irénée drew up the financial plan of the company to the last detail, under the title of *Statement of the Bylaws for the Establishment of a Military and Hunting Gun Powder Works in the United States*. The mill was to have a capital of

$36,000, representing eighteen founders' shares at $2000 each. The family having taken twelve shares, there would be only six left. Two would be reserved if possible for American citizens. One of Pierre-Samuel's old friends, Duquesnoy, had subscribed and paid for one share, the Swiss financier Bidermann (already cited), M. Catoire and M. Necker (Mme. de Staël's uncle) had done likewise. It went without saying that Eleuthère-Irénée would manage the works. His salary would be fixed at $1800 a year. Shareholders would be paid at an interest rate of 6 per cent. Profits or losses would be shared, two-thirds by the shareholders, one-third by the manager. The following detail is significant insofar as it indicates what part, in Eleuthère-Irénée's eyes, the family should have in the control of the business: In case the manager should die, the du Ponts alone were to name his successor.

Among the little group of friends who often visited Bon Séjour, the house at Bergen Point, Eleuthère-Irénée's plan was liked so much that a list of contingent subscribers now had to be chosen. The final choice boiled down to two names, one a Philadelphia merchant, Archibald McCall, the other a French *émigré* who had become an American citizen, Pierre Bauduy de Bellevue, strongly recommended by Colonel Toussard. "Peter" Bauduy spoke and wrote English fluently. In addition, he was experienced in business and knew American law. And he had contrived to make himself so popular in Wilmington that it was to him, a man of cultivated taste driven out of Santo Domingo by the slave uprising of 1791, that the city had turned to draw up plans for a city hall.

The Colonel, whose idea the powder mill had been in the first place, obtained a promise that Bauduy would be named the firm's business manager.

At first, Eleuthère-Irénée, who would have preferred to modernize an existing mill rather than build a new one from scratch, made some overtures looking to the purchase of the William Lane and Stephen Decatur powder works in Frankford, Pennsylvania. But they could not come to terms. He then decided to travel through different regions and pick out a suitable location. After having visited the Washington, Philadelphia and New York areas, he returned to Bergen Point still unsatisfied, whereupon Peter Bauduy, who was also on the lookout, reported a farm for sale in Delaware which would apparently make an excellent site.

Eleuthère-Irénée left at once for Wilmington. He paid the place a visit and looked it over with the greatest care, then told Bauduy it exactly filled his needs. He put Bauduy in charge of negotiations with the owner, a Quaker by the name of Jacob Broom. On April 27, 1802, title was passed in the name of a certain William Hamon, a Frenchman by birth whose citizenship seemed less contestable than Bauduy's (Delaware being one of the states where foreigners could not own land).

When everything was in order, Eleuthère-Irénée, together with his wife and three children, left Bon Séjour for a long carriage trip over bad roads to settle on the land, 130 miles away, bought from Jacob Broom. The household furniture and the machinery were to be forwarded aboard the schooner *Betsy of Paterson*, which would land her cargo at the port of New Castle, eleven miles from what would be the powder mill.

Was Eleuthère-Irénée's wife Sophie dismayed when she saw the miserable abode where she was to live for the interim? Under other circumstances she had shown her courage, and now she proved one more time that she knew how to adapt to difficult situations. On February 7, 1803, Eleuthère-Irénée was able to write thus to his father, who had returned to France in 1802 to look for new capital: "We have built a large house, a stone shed and the largest part of the mill. We have cleaned up the watercourse and the sawmill where we are getting the wood ready for our timber-work. . . . We have three more mills to build this month, and must dig a millrace for the works, put up a drying shed, the magazines and the workers' quarters. It is evident that we shall not be able to make powder before the fall."

Eleuthère-Irénée was only a few weeks off the mark in his forecast. Actually, the work had proceeded faster than he had calculated; and in July, 1803, he proudly finished his first batch of saltpeter. He wrote to President Jefferson to apprise him of the event. Jefferson, through the Secretary of War, had him assigned a small order for the Army of the United States.

While these events were taking place on the rocky banks of the Brandywine River, what had become of the other members of the family? Victor had returned from France in February, 1802, without having found any sleeping partners for his firm. Bureaux de Pusy, who had followed him to Europe, had become no less unhappy and disgusted with the American adventure. He had accepted a position offered him in France and his wife had gone there to rejoin him. His departure from the company of du Pont de Nemours, father and sons (which had hardly existed except on paper), had a bad effect on the shareholders, certain of whom seized on this pretext to withdraw their support. But for the faith of Pierre-Samuel, who heroically defended the firm's existence, however illusory, the whole enterprise would probably have been liquidated. He decided to leave immediately for France and try himself to organize new financing. Pierre-Samuel had an extraordinary *Monsieur Prudhomme* side to his nature. Henri Monnier could have put this declaration made by Pierre-Samuel in 1801 straight into the mouth of his hero, that carica-ture of the French bourgeois: "The son of my youth I called Victor, but the son of my maturity [*raison*] I called Eleuthère-Irénée. . . . The 'peaceful friend of liberty' [translation of the name Eleuthère] hopes, when making gunpowder, that it will never be used for war, but only in war's preservative exercises. . . ."

He also had a practical business side, however, as already evidenced by the way he extolled the products his sons would manufacture. It was thanks to him, without doubt, that Jefferson saw to it that Irénée's little company got its first government order. Pierre-Samuel's support of the company was to become even more useful in the months to come. "I hope," he wrote to Jefferson from Paris in 1803, "that you do not have your powder made nor your saltpeter refined anywhere but in my mill. (1) It is incomparably the best there is in the United States and one of the best in the world; (2) your old-fashioned powders need to be 'reshuffled'; (3) it is [made by] your faithful friend. . . ."

When Jefferson received this pressing letter of self-recommendation, he had his reasons for not displeasing his "faithful friend." Since June, 1802, Pierre-Samuel had been in Paris, where he had been confidentially commissioned by the President of the United States to act as intermediary between the American government and the First Consul in negotiating the cession of Louisiana to this country.

Pierre-Samuel, prior to sailing for France on May 5, 1802, aboard the Benjamin Franklin, had received the following letter from Jefferson:

[70]

Washington April 25, 1802

Dear Sir,

The week being now closed, during which you have given me a hope of seeing you here, I think it safe to enclose you my letters for Paris, lest they should fail of the benefit of so desirable a conveyance. . . . I wish you to be possessed of the subject, because you may be able to impress on the government of France the inevitable consequences of their taking possession of Louisiana; and though, as I here mention, the cession of New Orleans and the Floridas to us would be a palliation, yet I believe it would be no more, and that this measure would cost France, and perhaps not very long hence, a war which will annihilate her on the ocean, and place that element under the despotism of two nations, which I am not reconciled to more because my own would be one of them. And to this the exclusive appropriation of both continents of America as a consequence. I wish the present order of things to continue, and with a view to this I value highly a state of friendship between France and us. You know too well how sincere I have ever been in the dispositions to doubt them. You know, too, how much I value peace, and how unwillingly I should see an event take place which would render war a necessary recourse; and that all our movements should change their character and object. I am thus open with you, because I trust that you will have in your power to impress on that government considerations, in the scale against which the possession of Louisiana is nothing. In Europe, nothing but Europe is seen, or supposed to have any right in the affairs of nations; but this little event, of France's possessing herself of Louisiana, which is thrown in as nothing as a mere make-weight in a general settlement of accounts, — this speck which now appears as an almost invisible point in the horizon, is the embryo of a tornado which will burst on the countries on both sides of the Atlantic, and involve in its effects their highest destinies. That it may be avoided is my sincere prayer; and if you can be the means of informing the wisdom of Bonaparte of all its consequences, you have deserved well of both countries. Peace and abstinence from European interference are our objects, and so will continue while the present order of things in America remains uninterrupted.

Long an intimate friend of Talleyrand, du Pont *père* was certainly in an excellent position to make Napoleon understand the advantage to be gained from a transaction made on a friendly basis. The French expedition to Santo Domingo had failed. This meant that France lacked a secure base to serve as a relay point between the homeland and New Orleans. If the Americans wanted to take Louisiana by force, it would be difficult to prevent them. This immense region, discovered by La Salle in 1682, was only loosely identified with the state of Louisiana as known today. For a long time it actually had been a French colony, but only since 1800 had it been formally ceded to France by Spain through the secret Treaty of San Ildefonso. When informed of this treaty, Jefferson had not hesitated for an instant. "On all the earth there is only one place where the owner might be our natural enemy," he had written to Robert Livingston, his ambassador at Paris. "This place is New Orleans. . . . Therefore, we must marry the United States to the British fleet and nation." Had Jefferson, like his predecessor Adams, forgotten services rendered by France to the American colonies when they were fighting against England for their independence? It seems that debts of gratitude are nowhere in this world eternal! Had he also forgotten the Treaty of Perpetual Alliance signed February 6, 1778, by the United States? On the American side it was possible to claim that the treaty had lapsed the day Louis XVI was guillotined, since it was the "Very Christian King," and not France as a whole, who had been involved.

Moreover, the President had excuses for using menacing language. During the period between the signing of the Treaty of San Ildefonso and France's actually taking possession of Louisiana, an "incident" had occurred. The Spanish governor had announced his intention of closing to American shipping the port of New Orleans, which commanded entry to the hinterland all the way to the Great Lakes. This threat infuriated people living in the interior. They told Jefferson that unless he did something about it, they would take matters into their own hands and lay siege to the city. Being a realist, Napoleon recognized that it would be better to "let things go, before they let go of us," and named his price. Pierre-Samuel from the wings and Monroe from the center of the stage were the artificers of the Treaty of 1803, which sanctioned the cession of Louisiana to

America by Napoleon. They had come to terms at 15 million dollars. The American emissaries, who had come to negotiate only the purchase of New Orleans and a part of Florida, had acquired without previous intent an immense territory double the area of the original states. Talleyrand was not wrong when he smilingly said to them: "You've made a good deal." Coming from him, *"une bonne affaire"* made a lot of sense. And it also made a lot of sense to the practical people of the new republic, and to Jefferson in particular, since in 1804, thanks to the Louisiana Purchase, his popularity had become so great that he was re-elected President by a tremendous majority.

Before going back to France in 1802, Pierre-Samuel had thought it might be a good idea to reorganize his business affairs in America, and accordingly had divided them up into three distinct departments:

1. *Victor du Pont & Co.*, registered offices in the city of New York. Capital: the Bon Séjour property in New Jersey, plus 20 acres and a workshop in Alexandria, Virginia, and 6000 additional acres in the same state.

2. *Wilmington (Del.) Powder Co.*, with a majority of capital held by the du Ponts.

3. *Du Pont de Nemours (Père et Fils & Co.)*, registered offices in Paris, with an affiliate in New York and 6000 French acres (7500 American acres) of land in Kentucky.

But reorganization was only part of the problem. The other was to capitalize all these enterprises. The need for capital was so great, in fact, that Victor, manager of Victor du Pont & Co., came up with the idea of bringing an agent of the French government by the name of Pichon into the various combinations. Pichon had come to New York to try to arrange the shipment from the United States of provisions for the French expeditionary force into Santo Domingo commanded by General Leclerc, Bonaparte's brother-in-law. Leclerc, who had known the older du Pont son for years and who had every confidence in him, for equally good reason had no faith at all in Pichon. Schemer that he was, one day Pichon introduced Victor to Bonaparte's youngest brother, Jerome, who at the age of nineteen had just committed a great piece of folly by deserting the battleship to which he had been assigned by Bonaparte and then, on top of that, marrying a young Baltimorean, Elizabeth Patterson, eighteen years old and famous both for her beauty and for the daring gowns she wore to reveal her charms.

According to French law, this marriage was null and void, for Jerome Bonaparte was a minor. It could have been legally contracted only with his mother's consent, a detail which was plainly lacking.

Leclerc having died of the same yellow fever that had decimated his army, it may have been that Victor du Pont believed he had hit on a favorable opportunity to win new support from Napoleon. Or possibly Victor's wife gave him bad advice, being bored with New York and dreaming of having her husband return to France to make a career for himself in diplomacy. The latter is certainly possible. Reading Mme. Victor du Pont's *Memoirs,* it is clearly evident that she wished that her husband, instead of sailing from La Rochelle to America in 1799, had accepted the post of consul-general of France at Naples as proposed for him by his friend the French General Clarke, who had just been named Ambassador to that city. In any event, Napoleon had forbidden French officials to lend money to his youngest brother. By this he hoped to bring the young wastrel to his knees. However, Victor unwisely helped Jerome, and Napoleon got wind of it almost as soon as he was tipped off about Pichon's dishonesties. Leclerc was no longer around to clear Victor. Napoleon reacted in the spirit of a man about to become emperor. The unfortunate Victor's name henceforth was classified, once and for all, as among those best never even uttered in Bonaparte's presence.*

All this was well known in informed Paris and New York circles. The Victor du Pont Co. of New York went bankrupt in 1805, and Victor departed the city to run

---

* After his marriage to Elizabeth Patterson had been annulled, and despite the fact he had had a child from this hasty union, Jerome married Princess Catherine of Württemberg. It is one of Jerome's descendants whom French Bonapartists regard as the candidate for an eventual imperial restoration.

a farm in Angelica, in western New York. There he spent three miserable years, unable to earn enough money to pay his debts. At last, in 1809, he accepted his younger brother's invitation to come with his family — he had two sons and his wife was expecting — and live near Eleuthère on the banks of the Brandywine.

Of all the du Pont undertakings, the powder works was the only one that offered hope of success. Though there was no doubt Eleuthère-Irénée was making a go of it, his powder mill was beset at first by innumerable difficulties. At the very beginning he had become clearly aware of the inconvenience of having to depend so heavily on the intelligent but overly aggressive Peter Bauduy. True enough, it was thanks to Bauduy's credit that Eleuthère-Irénée had been able to make a start, but he felt he had paid too dearly for the $8000 vouched for by this partner and too dearly also for the additional $18,000 which Bauduy secured by placing a mortgage on his Moncton Park property. This last amount was to buy up McCall's share and assure the company working capital. And in 1804, Eleuthère-Irénée was horrified that Bauduy had had the audacity to propose that the firm's name be changed to Du Pont, Bauduy & Co. "If, as I hope," the indignant younger du Pont had replied, "this company gains a reputation greater than all others, and if it makes a name for itself, this will be done in my name." And it was in fact his own name

that Lavoisier's pupil had given the powder works —
he called it the Eleutherian Mills — as additionally wit-
nessed by this announcement which appeared in a New
York newspaper in 1804:

E. I. DU PONT DE NEMOURS
GUNPOWDER MANUFACTORY
Wilmington, Delaware
This new and extensive establishment is now in activity
and any quantity of powder, equal if not superior to any
manufactured in Europe, will be delivered at shortest notice.
Samples to be seen at V. DU PONT DE NEMOURS, NEW YORK.

After 1805, unfortunately, it was no longer possible,
as we have noted, to see samples of Wilmington powder in New York, Victor having by this time shut up
shop. Nevertheless, despite this handicap the fact remained that Irénée's company was forging ahead, for
in 1805 it did $46,857.75 worth of business, compared
to $15,116.75 the year before.

In 1811, through a letter from their father, who had
remained in France since 1802, the du Pont sons in
Wilmington learned of three developments which disturbed them very much. First, Du Pont de Nemours
Père et Fils et Cie in Paris had also gone into bank-
ruptcy. Second, Pierre-Samuel had offered to reimburse
the stockholders with shares that the company held in
the powder mill. Finally, he had borrowed money from

several of his friends, including 100,000 francs from Talleyrand. But there is nothing surprising about the fact that the name of Talleyrand, Prince of Benevent, should be involved in the hazardous beginnings of the Du Pont Company. Talleyrand was a man who had his finger in all sorts of pies. Shamefully mercenary, he had the reputation of even making a good thing on the side out of the treaties he negotiated in the name of France. It is even said that he tried to get — and may actually have obtained — a commission from the American plenipotentiaries who came to bargain in Paris for the purchase of Louisiana. Napoleon despised his minister, while making use of him for the reason that he was indispensable. Talleyrand was everywhere, even mixed up in Du Pont combines through one of his henchmen, Ménestrier. Only this man's name is found signed to a certain act of agreement in the du Pont Library. This historic document deals with "a loan in cash for the business needs of Sieur Du Pont, vice-president of the Chamber of Commerce, living on Rue de Provence, Paris." The loan will be paid "in 12 bills payable to bearer spaced out to December 31, 1813." The intermediary in the arrangement is Jean Victor Auguste Ménestrier, who "lives at 83 Rue St. Honoré, Paris." Talleyrand, to say the least, had shown a lack of flair in letting slip through his fingers a chance to own a part of the du Pont enterprise. He had taken pains, as a matter of fact, to specify that "the business at hand does not involve investment

. . . but solely a personal obligation to Sieur du Pont."
This personal obligation, however, was hedged round
by precautions, Talleyrand having exacted as guarantee
a mortgage on the Brandywine gunpowder mill. There
is great wealth to this day at Château de Valençay,
where, after recent litigation, those heirs permitted to
use the name of Talleyrand were legally determined.
But they would all have been very much richer had
Napoleon's clever minister not contented himself with
limiting his investment to a meager 5 per cent interest
on the money lent.

To get back to the elder du Pont's letter, the sons'
main concern was that the company founded by
Eleuthère-Irénée, because of Pierre-Samuel's promises,
might be in danger of passing into the hands of strangers. They also dreaded the possibility that if the Wilmington enterprise should look too good as seen from
afar, the people owning shares in the powder mill
might demand payment of their money at a time when
the cash-box held only enough to carry on production
from one day to the next. But the dreaded possibility
happened. In 1812 Bureaux de Pusy's widow (Pierre-
Samuel's stepdaughter), accompanied by her two
daughters, arrived without a word of warning in Wilmington. She had inherited a share and a half in the
company and now demanded $20,000 on the spot! The
two brothers refused to pay her off. Infuriated by this
rebuff, she went to Philadelphia and wrote to her step-

father that his sons were crooks. Meanwhile she brought Peter Bauduy into the picture. Because he was still trying to get his hands on the powder works, he confirmed the lady's accusations in a letter to the shareholders. Duquesnoy and Bidermann asked Pierre-Samuel to explain, and he in turn sent a reproachful letter to his children, in which he said they were "unworthy of the name they bore." During this period Ferdinand Bauduy, Peter's son, who had married Victorine, Eleuthère-Irénée's oldest daughter, died. As a result there were no more family ties between the Bauduys and the du Ponts. The two brothers now made it plain to their business manager that he was not going to be kept on. Bauduy, in short, had failed to make good his bid. He withdrew, selling them his two shares, but himself founded a powder mill on his old Moncton Park property in competition with the du Ponts! This firm did not close its doors until 1861.

To find out what was really going on, Bidermann sent his son James-Antoine on a trip to Wilmington. This elegant young man of twenty-one not only cleared the du Ponts of unjust accusations, but also asked his father for permission to stay on in Wilmington, where he had been offered the post vacated by Peter Bauduy. Having become tied in with the firm, some years later he went one step further and became a member of the family by marrying Eveline, Eleuthère-Irénée's second daughter. Thus were familial storms appeased, while in Europe, where Pierre-Samuel was still residing, a mightier tempest was unleashed.

In April, 1814, Russian Cossacks and Prussian Uhlans were camping in the Champs Élysées in Paris. As positively as in olden times when he had been a partisan of the Revolution, Pierre-Samuel now longed for the downfall of Napoleon's dictatorial régime. The certain belief had arisen in France that the wily Talleyrand had long since been preparing for this eventuality. It was all quite natural, therefore, that Talleyrand should choose du Pont as secretary of the provisional government, set up under agreement with the Tsar, to liquidate Napoleon's imperial régime.

The disillusioned old man of seventy-five, in April, 1815, some weeks after Napoleon's return from Elba, wrote to Jean-Baptiste Say: "I am writing you as I go to America so as not to be passed from hand to hand like a bootlicker or a whore [*comme un courtisan ou une courtisane*]." He wanted to return to America, which would be his first trip back since he left in 1802.

In this fashion the family was to be almost completely reunited again. The only ones missing from those who had gathered fifteen years before at Bon Séjour were Mme. Pierre-Samuel du Pont, who had sustained a fall just at the moment when the ship was to set sail and had stayed at Le Havre; Bureaux de Pusy, who was dead; and Pusy's abusive widow, whose jeremiads had exasperated Pierre-Samuel.

When the head of the family arrived in the United States, Victor du Pont changed his plans. His wife, who most decidedly had not been adjusting to Wilmington, had made up her mind that Napoleon's abdication had cleared away her husband's last reasons for not returning to Paris. The Bourbons would undoubtedly want to draw on the talents of the exiled. What was to prevent Victor from putting himself at the disposal of King Louis XVIII? She convinced Victor sufficiently for him to allow her to book passage on a ship to France. He would join her there after straightening out his affairs in America. It had all been settled and Mme. Victor was waiting to go aboard her ship in Philadelphia when, at the beginning of April, 1815, it was suddenly reported that Pierre-Samuel had left Le Havre in March on the *Fingal*. It went without saying that she would now wait for her father-in-law.

During Pierre-Samuel's long absence his family had grown so much that the newcomers more than made up for the missing ones. When his father had left for Paris, Victor had had only two children; now he had three. Little Julia-Sophie had been born near Wilmington in 1806. At Eleuthère-Irénée's, the three children whom Pierre-Samuel had known had now been augmented by three more, Eleuthera, Sophie-Madeleine and Henry, all born, like Julia-Sophia, on the banks of the Brandywine. Still another child, Alexis, would be born in 1816. Finally, Victor's oldest daughter, already wed, had made Pierre-Samuel a great-grandfather by giving birth to a daughter, Gabrielle-Josephine.

Business changes were just as great. On May 19, 1815, carried away by enthusiasm, Pierre-Samuel wrote to his wife in France: "I have seen the manufactory. It is gigantic, inconceivable that only one man was able to design and execute such things, especially this hydraulic machinery and these mechanical devices. . . . Irénée is a great man, with talent, courage, perseverance ten times greater than I had ever dared hope, although I have always held him in high esteem. Charles [Victor's oldest son, born in 1797] has grown up into an intelligent young man, a good and solid nature. It is he who is in charge of the spinning mill. Alfred [Eleuthère-Irénée's oldest son, born in 1798] is a little slow, but he is interested in mathematics and shows promise of becoming somebody, one way or another. . . ."

Pierre-Samuel had only a very little time left to live in the bosom of his family. Month after month, despite his wife's pleading, he put off going back to France. The old man was happy among his children and grandchildren and his faithful friends. He was deeply attached to America, which in his eyes was the democratic Republic he had always dreamed of. No question but that he dreaded, having rediscovered America, what was waiting for him in Paris: ". . . a monarchic régime

[84]

tinged with clericalism, dominated by the ghosts of a condemned epoch," and the presence of the odious stepdaughter who had embroiled him with his sons.

As it was, he already regretted having brought along with him to Wilmington, as secretary, Maurice Bureaux, one of his wife's nephews, who turned out to be very unpleasant and whom everybody could hardly wait to see leave again for France.

On February 6, 1816, Pierre-Samuel wrote to one of his friends: "It is one of my incurable ills that wherever I go, I make work for myself. The closer I come to death, the more determined I am not to rest until the day after I am buried. . . ." His excessive activity was indeed one of his faults. It augmented the gout that constantly tormented him as well as the disabilities of old age. On August 5, 1817, a fire broke out near the powder works and he absolutely insisted in joining his family in the bucket brigade carrying water from the Brandywine to help put out the flames. Exhausted by the effort, the next day he had to stay in bed. He died on the 8th. Jefferson wrote to his sons: "A beloved friend, a patriot and an upright man has died." He was buried near by the Eleutherian Mills, on his private land where someday he would be surrounded by his family.

4

The Brandywine

Fervet opus . . .
Virgil
Georgics, IV, 169

"IT IS EIGHT OR TEN YEARS," we are told in a copy of
the Baltimore *Evening Post* of 1810, "since the du
Pont de Nemours bought their gullied site, half-covered
with rocks, on the Brandywine. Now it flourishes like
the rose. Once naked hills are clothed in verdure and
covered with flocks. Eleuthère-Irénée has built a charming village and nearby, the powder works. Now he is
busy constructing a wool spinning mill which soon will
be going full blast. He is the region's benefactor, loved
by the numerous artisans he employs."

Victor and Irénée, very different though they were
in character, were extremely fond of each other. This
mutual attachment had to be very strong for Eleuthère-
Irénée, heavily burdened by family as he was, to have
his older brother, all of whose attempts to get along had
failed, come to live near him, and for Victor to accept

[86]

such an invitation without any feeling of jealousy.

The establishment of an agricultural colony with allied industries had figured prominently in Pierre-Samuel's original plan. The idea of exploiting the land was still being considered in 1801, as attested by the fact — earlier noted — that Merino sheep were to be imported into America. The curious history of these Merinos is to be found in an article in the *Archives of Useful Knowledge,* published from 1810 to 1813 by James Mease. Pierre-Samuel's friend, the banker Delessert, during the Revolution in France had been able to preserve intact almost his entire flock of Merinos. In 1796 the Directoire had sent him, in the role of expert, to Spain to select 4000 Merino sheep for delivery to the French under the terms of the Treaty of Basel. Delessert conscientiously carried out his assignment. However, he also made a good thing out of it by retaining a certain number of animals for his own use as breeding stock. Among these sheep was an exceptionally fine ram that he called Don Pedro. This ram was part of the lot that the banker had agreed to ship, upon his request, to Pierre-Samuel in New Jersey. Under the supervision of Eleuthère-Irénée, Don Pedro and three other stud rams were put aboard the *Benjamin Franklin,* sailing from the port of Le Havre in 1801. It had been agreed that Don Pedro would first be loaned to the du Ponts, then taken to a farm that Delessert had bought in Rosendale, near Kingston-on-Hudson in New York State; also that one of the other rams should be presented to Jefferson. These projects were upset when the *Benjamin Franklin* was captured by an English vessel and not released until three weeks later. Only Don Pedro, evidently the strongest, survived the confinement and crossing. Victor went to New York to pick up the animal, and Don Pedro was put out to graze at Bon Séjour. There he covered nine ewes and was then shipped, as agreed, to Rosendale. In 1805, when the Delessert property was put up for sale, the flock was broken up. The farmers thereabouts, who had little idea of the value of these sheep with the heavy tails, bought them at distress prices. Robert Livingston, who had heard of this sale through his friend Victor, made haste to get hold of a certain number of the sheep, which he added to his flock of purebreds stemming from Rambouillet, near Paris. Eleuthère-Irénée himself bought Don Pedro for $60. He brought him to the shores of the Brandywine where grazed the descendants of the ewes covered by him in 1801. Still "very active," Don Pedro did not die until 1811. It was evidently this same flock, which had been considerably increased thanks to his "activities," that the Baltimore newspaper writer had in mind when he wrote his article in 1810.

The memory of this ardent stud has not been forgotten in Wilmington. A wooden statue of him *au naturel* has been carefully preserved. This statue is provided with an opening into which oil is poured from time to time to protect the wood against drying out. What is probably a replica of this statue is standing today in Mrs. E. Paul du Pont's garden. The copy was made, it is said, on order by Pierre Bauduy, while associated with the spinning mill, as an ornament for the entrance to Eden Park, the Moncton Park property bought by Bauduy from the Count de Ségur, Lafayette's uncle. Bauduy also invested in Merino sheep to such an extent that he imported a sheperd and his dog from the Pyrenees to guard them.

In 1809, when Victor went to rejoin his brother in Delaware, Eleuthère-Irénée certainly had the intention of using this fine flock of sheep as the basis for establishing Victor in a mill for the manufacture of woolen goods. But could he have seriously imagined at the time that Victor could make a go of a woolen mill as he, Irénée, was doing with the powder works? Or was he motivated, without any great expectations, simply by a sincere desire to help his brother? The fact remains that on June 19, 1810, a contract drawn up in French was signed at the Eleutherian Mills by E. I. du Pont, Victor, Peter Bauduy and Raphael Duplanty to "form a company for the purpose of establishing on the Brandywine a cloth manufactory under the name of the Merino Wool Factory."

This mill was built with capital lent by Peter Bauduy on a site that was given the name of Louviers, in honor of the French town of the same name where then famous woolen mills were located. It opened its doors in July, 1811. Meanwhile, the firm charged with carrying out this enterprise had become Du Pont, Bauduy & Co. Their trademark showed two winged Indians crowned with plumes, one of whom was riding a Merino ram equipped with all masculine attributes. Above was an American eagle showing his claws.

In December of this opening year the Louviers weavers buckled down to a particularly important job. Victor had put them to work making cloth of a quality fit for tailoring into elegant garments. Later, as gifts, bolts were graciously given to the influential personages of the Republic, such as President Madison, Secretary of State Monroe and General Mason. The company thought that if it could be shown that the American Louviers was able to make a product comparable to that made in the French Louviers, in all likelihood the orders would come pouring in. Always optimistic like his father, Victor had made a trip through several states to get an advance check on the wool supply, and was already talking about setting up a second factory in the outskirts of Washington. But time did not confirm Victor's vision of the future. However, several farmers who up to that time had limited themselves to growing wheat — Delaware wheat sent to the millers of the Brandywine had a great reputation — responded to du Pont initiative by taking up sheep-raising. A sheep census taken in the area in 1812 showed there were some 4300 animals, of which 700 were purebred Merinos and 2000 crossbred.

In 1812, during the war with England, Louviers, which had been enlarged, was indeed overwhelmed with work; cloth for the troops was made there. But it appears that once hostilities had ceased, the mistake was made of not sticking to manufacture of standard-grade goods. The evil genius responsible for this error, it seems, was an Englishman who called himself William Clifford and who claimed to be the son of a rich textile manufacturer in England. He had married Amelia, Victor du Pont's second daughter. Amelia was not a good-looking girl, and her father was under no illusion about her attractiveness. He had probably been glad to get her married off. However, no one in the family except Amelia had any fondness for Clifford. It was on the advice of this supposed expert that it was decided to change over from the manufacture of ordinary cloth to fine woolens. Alas, Amelia had been married only three months when, normal relations with London having been re-established, it was discovered that Clifford was not his real name at all, that he was not rich and that he already had a wife at home. Without making a fuss about this annoying incident, the family got rid of the adventurer in 1814. His departure left the Louviers spinning mill without a manager as well as without enough customers.

The first manager, Ferdinand Bauduy, was already dead by 1813, leaving his wife Victorine du Pont a widow after only three months of marriage. When this came to pass, as we have already noted, a break occurred between Bauduy, father of the unfortunate Ferdinand, and the du Pont brothers. The Louviers spinning mills were losing money steadily, and finally shut down. But their brief existence must be noted, if only to underscore the fact that the du Ponts from the very start directed their affairs toward the two areas where they were eventually to make a fortune: the fields of textiles and of chemistry.

When, in 1801, Eleuthère-Irénée returned to Essonnes accompanied by Commissar Robin, he verified the fact that gunpowder, just as in his student days there with Lavoisier, was still being made of 76 parts of saltpeter, 14 of sulphur and 10 of charcoal. However, the mixture was now manufactured according to improved techniques, notably in grinding with fuller's earth and in the sifting process. Since 1788 Lavoisier had dreamed, after Berthollet's experiments, of replacing saltpeter, which was rare in France, with potassium chlorate. But an accident had occurred in which a number of people were killed, and Lavoisier had concluded it would be better to go back to saltpeter and make out by refining it more thoroughly to improve the quality of the end product. In 1792 he published a memoir "on different methods proposed for determining the titer or quality of raw saltpeter."*

Lavoisier substituted for the empiric method of manufacture a rational one. The progress which this brought about is attested by the fact that the French government thereafter forbade citizens without scientific training from carrying on saltpeter refining operations. That Lavoisier got results from his methods is beyond doubt: "National gunpowder," formerly "the King's gunpowder," during the wars of the Revolution had a carrying power of 115 to 130 toises (one toise equals 6.4 feet) as against 70 to 90 toises for other European powders. Irénée returned to Delaware with machinery designed by Essonnes engineers and at the same time brought back not only the secret process — improved even more since Lavoisier — for refining saltpeter but also a safety program for the pulverizing sheds.

A description of these times is given us by a lady who lived in Wilmington:

About the year 1800, the Messrs. Dupont & Co. made their first purchase here, that caused rumors to float through the country. The farmer was at his wit's end to conjecture what schemes were in view. To buy a barren tract of rocks! why, to expend cart-loads of money would not fit it for tillage. Others pitied the strangers for wasting their substance in wild adventure, and when the blasting of rocks

* This capital work was published in *Annales de Chimie*.

commenced, said, it will surely exhaust a mint! Yet many of those farmers lived to witness mighty obstacles surmounted; and their wise predictions to fail. Neighboring estates have been enhanced in value; neither has ruin befallen the projectors.

There was no house to be had near, and Mr. Dupont fitted up a cottage for the family, in which they resided. It was as common for snakes to crawl to and drink out of the water bucket as it would be in a backwood's cabin. What a transition to those persons, from the beauties and refinements of France, to the rugged woody heights and snaky rocks of Brandywine!

It is said that Mr. E. J. [*sic*] Dupont's house was built of the stone from a single rock, on the spot where it stands. This house is beautifully situated on the brow of a hill. As you descend by the road, suddenly it bursts upon the sight, adorned by clusters of forest trees left on either side. From a balcony you overlook the powder-yard and mills. Here hundreds of men are as actively engaged as the little busy bees providing their winter stores.*

This impression was attested by others, who told how the local masons among themselves made fun of the Frenchmen who were such fools as to have them build odd buildings with doors toward the stream and located close to the water which heretofore had served so usefully to turn the water wheels of grist- and paper-mills. They did not understand that when Irénée insisted so strongly on having very light roofs and only three

* Elizabeth Montgomery, *Reminiscences of Wilmington* (1851), p. 46.

thick walls it was to ensure, in case of explosion, that the blast would be vented upward and out toward the stream. A similar precaution would have prevented the total devastation of the explosion which destroyed the first powder mill built in America, at Milton, Massachusetts.

In fact, Irénée had decided to buy the property in the first place precisely because of its situation between river and hill. Irénée had also calculated that the Brandywine would provide him with all the power he needed to crush the powder by machine, while the magnificent willows on the property would supply excellent charcoal. Finally, the fact that Quaker Broom's old farm was isolated was all to the good for a powder works. At the same time, it was not too far from the highway going to Wilmington and New Castle, the latter a port on the Delaware River where cargoes of saltpeter coming from the Indies could be conveniently landed and whence barrels of gunpowder could be handily shipped to New York or to Washington, then about to become the capital of the United States. There was still another consideration: if it ever became necessary to expand, there would be no lack of space.

Among the equipment bought in France was a set of eprouvettes, as they are technically called, stubby bronze mortars used in testing the quality of gunpowder. If the product was of good quality, these eprouvettes, at an angle of 45 degrees and loaded with 92 grams (about 3.2 ounces) of powder, could send a ball weighing 29.4 kilograms (about 54.6 pounds) a distance of 225 meters (about 742 feet). A "perfect" powder would send the ball 250 meters. Pierre-Samuel had not exaggerated when he predicted to Jefferson that the Du Pont powders would be first-grade. Right from the start the Eleutherian Mills turned out a high-quality powder. Experts admired its slate-gray color, typical of the best gunpowders, the uniformity of its constituent grains and their "adequate resistance to being handled in transport." When a pinch of the Du Pont powder was burned on a piece of paper according to the classic test, not a trace of combustion showed, proving that the mixture had been precisely proportioned.

Every country has its bureaucracy, and democratic America was no exception. Despite Jefferson's backing and recommendations in favor of his old friend Pierre-Samuel, this bureaucracy was hard to jar out of its routine. Its habit was to get government gunpowder from certain suppliers, and it felt no inclination to look to the powder made by Du Pont. However, on July 4, 1805, after having learned of experiments made with the products of the Brandywine, General Dearborn, then Secretary of War, publicly declared that in the future the government would buy all its powder from Du Pont. But there was a big gap between word and deed.

It may be supposed that the vigilant lobbyists of the

time colored the attitude of the government bureaus. In January, 1808, Eleuthère-Irénée, in a letter to his father, accused no one, but simply said: "The secretaries employ me only when they can get no one else. . . . They have entrusted the refining of saltpeter to an apothecary who knows nothing about it at all, and who has spoiled the 90,000 pounds of it that the government turned over to him." The apothecary in question lived in Philadelphia.

Total gunpowder production that year, 1808, in the United States did not exceed 1.5 million pounds (including that coming from the Eleutherian Mills); and this total was not enough to meet the country's needs. What would happen if a new war broke out between the United States and England? From 1795 to 1809, the government had bought $214,000 worth of powder from American manufacturers, but Du Pont's share had not exceeded $30,000. This being the case, it is remarkable that Eleuthère-Irénée, with an eye to the future, should have taken it upon himself to stock up on saltpeter at the end of 1811. That same year, under the presidency of James Madison, a friend of Secretary of War William Eustis named Thomas Ewell proposed that Eleuthère-Irénée should tie up with him to obtain large government orders. Though he knew nothing about gunpowder manufacture, Ewell had set up a mill near Washington which, thanks to his "excellent connections," was swamped with work!

Eleuthère-Irénée refused to enter into this convenient association and had the courage to publish a pamphlet entitled *Villainy Detected,* exposing the deals of Thomas Ewell. In the end he had no reason to regret it; for in 1812 war came with England and the panicky government immediately assigned him an order for 200,000 pounds of gunpowder. In 1813 he got another order for 500,000 more.

Even working at full capacity the mill was not up to furnishing such large quantities. It would have to be expanded. But this entailed risk. If hostilities ceased, what good would the supplementary powder sheds be? If America lost the war, who would pay for the powder already ordered? Bauduy, the company's business manager, advised Eleuthère-Irénée to be cautious. Irénée was of just the opposite opinion. Mortgaging the property, he raised $46,000, which he used to buy the neighboring farm of Hagley, belonging to a rich Philadelphia merchant, Rumford Dawes, who had been using it as a summer place. This purchase is worth noting, for it marked the start of Du Pont's expansionist policy.

The first two years of the war seemed to confirm Bauduy's opinion. The American Army, meager and poorly trained on account of the pacifist Jefferson administration's failure to provide adequate funds, not only was unable to take Canada, but even allowed the English to occupy some United States territory.

In 1813 a British fleet came to anchor at New Castle,

Delaware. People began to wonder whether the Du Pont powder works might not be captured. On this occasion Victor distinguished himself at the head of a company of Delaware militia, comprising 7448 effectives. It is said that it was the bravery of these militiamen which persuaded the commander of the English expedition to take to the sea. The du Ponts escaped unscathed from what could have been disaster, but the United States as a whole was to know some tragic hours. In 1814 English vessels reached the mouth of the Potomac. Contingents of the regular American army, charged with fighting the enemy expeditionary corps, melted away. President Madison, who had succeeded Jefferson in 1809, had just barely time to flee the White House before the invaders burned it to the ground in reprisal for useless destruction visited by the Americans on York (now Toronto) in Canada.

The American command was thrown back on its heels by this sudden attack. The government suffered a crisis. Though the Eleutherian Mills were working harder than ever, payments from the Treasury arrived either late or not at all. The banks in several of the states, including those of New England, were paying only a part of their bills in cash. But then the wind shifted. American victories, above all one on Lake Champlain, coupled with the lassitude of the English, led the British government to sue for peace. The treaty was signed at Ghent in December, 1814.

The dire consequences of peace to Du Pont were immediately realized at Eleutherian Mills, where $125,-000 had been invested in expansion, the purchase of raw material and other goods. Eleuthère-Irénée had only $10,000 in ready cash, and the government was not paying its debts.

Nor was it easy to borrow from local bankers because, according to M. de la Rochefoucault-Liancourt, during this period there were only three banks in all of Delaware, and all three of them together had a capital of only $550,000. It is not hard to imagine that they were in no position to supply Du Pont with the liquid capital it so desperately needed at the end of each month. Du Pont's first participation in an American war had not proved especially profitable on the bookkeeping level. Still, it had had two results which could not help but sweeten the future:

(1) By nearly doubling their productive capacity between 1812 and 1814 they had definitely become the main powder-makers in the United States.

(2) And by taking part in the defense of their new country, Eleuthère-Irénée and Victor had overcome once and for all the prejudice against them as foreigners. Henceforth they would never be known as anything but "true Americans."

Pierre-Samuel's arrival at Wilmington in 1815, as we have seen, had changed the plans of Victor du Pont and his family just when they were on the verge of going back to France. This indicates that even after the War of 1812 Mme. Victor had no desire to stay in America. However, she had to resign herself to this fate. In June, 1815, Victor ran for the office of state representative in the Delaware Assembly and was elected. If Victor shared his father's agnostic views, it would be interesting to know what went through his mind when he was repeating the constitutional oath of office: "I declare my belief in God the Father, in Jesus Christ His only Son and in the Holy Ghost, one God indivisible, forever blessed. And I recognize the Scriptures of the Old and New Testaments as having been given by divine inspiration." Victor's new duties obliged him to settle with his family in Dover, the state capital. In 1817 Victor moved up from the lower chamber to the State Senate, where he served until 1824.

Though in 1815 the powder mills were in an embarrassing financial situation, their business volume at least had considerably increased. Production now surpassed the 1812 figures by 75,000 pounds (which goes to prove that in times of peace the pioneer American people had a growing need for gunpowder), but funds at the disposal of the company treasury continued as always to be in short supply. That in itself must have been a source of concern for a precise man like Eleuthère-Irénée. This difficulty now became compounded by a serious mishap. In 1815, for the first time in its thirteen years of existence, the Eleutherian Mills had a bad accident, in which nine workers were killed and $20,000 worth of damage was inflicted. Du Pont finances must have still been in a bad way in 1817, since in the Archives of Longwood there is the rough draft of a letter from Victor to Stephen Girard, an old Bordeaux seaman who had made an enormous fortune in Philadelphia,* which begins:

Monsieur, an unforeseen event and one that could be disastrous for us by ruining our credit forces us to turn to you as perhaps the only person who may be able to relieve our financial difficulties, and although we have little claim on your kindness, your character is too well known for us to hesitate in believing that by proposing a business deal to you in which all manner of security would be offered, you will be induced to give us preference by virtue of the good that will come of it for a numerous and respectable family of compatriots. . . .

---

* Many Frenchmen came to the United States during the French Revolution, and a great many of them preferred not to return to France even after the advent of the Empire. A certain number became firmly fixed in Wilmington. According to the memoirs of the period, among this last group, which included of course the Bauduys, the Hamons and Colonel Toussard, were: a son-in-law of Bauduy named Garesché, descended from an old Calvinist family of La Rochelle; John James Ullmann, a Strasbourg Jew and a former pupil, like Eleuthère-Irénée, of Lavoisier, who made a fortune in a dyeworks business; Dr. Didier, Mr. de Provenchères, the Marquise de la Source (or Sourci?); and Mr. Deschapelles (or de la Chapelle), all of whom had come either directly from France or from Santo Domingo at the time of the slave revolt. Also, the future King Louis-Philippe used to come to take English lessons in Wilmington during his Philadelphia exile. Stephen Girard had settled in Philadelphia before the French Revolution. He died in 1831, leaving $7,500,000 to charity.

There is no indication, however, that Girard personally lent money to the du Ponts, but it was very probably he who interceded on their behalf with William Warner of Philadelphia and got him to advance them, with all guarantees that might be desired, the $30,000 that got them off the hook. The debt to Warner was not entirely paid up until April, 1823. One notes that the Physiocrat's old personal debt to Talleyrand was not settled until 1829 and then only after the insistence of the prince's American agents, Le Roy, Bayard and Co. of New York. This indicates that the du Ponts must have continued to have money troubles up to that year.

In 1818 the plant had an accident even worse than the one in 1815. Elizabeth Montgomery again tells us what took place.*

However feeble the effort, we will attempt briefly to portray the explosion in March, 1818. About ten o'clock the town was thrown into consternation. The noise burst upon the ear like the report of a cannon, and the earth shook! At the moment crossing King and Second Street, my attention was fixed on passengers hastening on to the steamboat. The earth trembled, my ear was stunned, and I involuntarily exclaimed, "The steamboat!" Many voices echoed, "Yes! Milnor's boat full of passengers is blown up!" Men and women ran to and fro. My steps were bent to a store in Second Street, where a friend was waiting for me. This family had assembled in the store, and said it was an earthquake, the windows shook and the door bell rang aloud.

* *Reminiscences of Wilmington*, p. 47.

We hastened homeward almost breathless, hearing on the way it was a magazine in rear of our dwellings, opposite the Town Hall. A second tremendous report seemed to lift us from our feet. Now we ascertained it was the powder-mills, by the dense black smoke rising in piles of clouds, and gathering into a column, fold upon fold, and twisting into a cork-screw shape, varying in lights and shades, stretched over our heads and seeming to totter as if ready to fall and crush all beneath. Some of the dark folds appeared bespangled with stars, others looked like brilliant clusters suspended and enveloped by a thin mist, shooting out and twinkling as they fell, till lost in the blaze of noonday. This scene was too magnificent for ordinary powers to portray.

Nearer home a horseman passed in full gallop, shouting "Raise your windows!" Another followed as rapidly and cried, "Abandon your houses, the grand magazine will soon explode." Every dwelling was quickly deserted, even by the domestic animals. Being about the hour to prepare dinner, some had meat on the fire, others had it spitted, and in the general confusion much was thrown on the floor, where it lay untouched for three hours at least.

Friends had assembled for worship, when the messenger gave the alarm; and as a rare occurrence they left the meeting-house in a body, and walked up the middle of the street. From the lower part of the town, not a few women and children fled across the Christiana. Men and boys, with some women, ran to the fatal spot. But a very large group of women and children, of every age, class and color, mingled on a vacant square on Market Street. Invalids who had not been out of their house all winter, and the aged and the infirm fled for shelter to a school-house with no chimney. The March wind blew keenly, yet none of these caught cold, so intense was the excitement.

Amid this great consternation, it might truly be called a noiseless day! Every voice was hushed, and all spoke in a whisper: no noisy mirth or crying of children disturbed the quiet sadness of the mixed multitude. The dog was subdued and ceased to bark, and so softened into sympathetic fear, couched at his owner's feet. Pacing of horses and footsteps were the only sound to interrupt the awful silence, while memory was refreshed with the descriptions read of earthquakes in by-gone days, when danger threatened; the people were seized with despair, and in profound silence waited the sad doom to be engulfed in the bowels of the earth.

Intense anxiety was depicted in each countenance to hear the true statement. At one o'clock, the thrilling story was told that instantaneously forty souls were hurled into an unknown eternity; and fragments of their mangled bodies were scattered over the face of the earth, or lodged on the tops of trees; that widows and orphans rent the air in wailing and lamentation, as they stood shuddering over the spot of this appalling tragedy.

By throwing a quantity of powder into the water, much destruction was arrested, and many lives preserved. It was extremely perilous to those engaged, and those whose foresight and energy had proposed it, among whom was Marshal Grouchy,* on a visit to the family. Of all the explosions, this one was the most terrific and fatal.

The bereavement of the widows awakened the sympathies of E. J. [*sic*] Dupont, Esq., and it was not a momentary impulse. He, with noble generosity, allowed to each

* This was the "Grouchy! It was Blücher" made famous by Victor Hugo's poem on the battle of Waterloo.

one an annuity during her widowhood, and this benevolence was faithfully fulfilled, and continued to the few who remained after he lay mouldering in the dust!

It was this benevolence which moved William Brooson to write in his *Agenda of 1825*: "E. I. Du Pont . . . is a remarkable man. To him must be attributed the development of the Brandywine Valley during the past 15 years. As a businessman he is surpassed by no one, I believe, in intelligence and imagination. As a member of the company he is universally respected for his generosity, his amiability and his integrity."

At this explosion, besides the forty casualties, there was $120,000 damage. Among the injured were Charles Dalmas, Eleuthère-Irénée's brother-in-law, and Irénée's wife Sophie, to whom he was as ever most romantically devoted. Irénée himself was in Philadelphia on a business trip; but Victor was on the scene and escaped death only by a miracle.

There was only one other industry of any importance in the Valley: a paper mill using an entirely new process to make paper out of old rags. This mill was not at all on the same scale as the Du Pont works which Eleuthère-Irénée managed and which manufactured 800,000 pounds of powder annually. He employed 140 hands. By present standards this does not seem like many but for that time it was considerable. Among the most important customers of the powder works was a former

German immigrant by the name of John Jacob Astor. Arriving in America in 1783, Astor had specialized in the fur trade; and it may be noted that from 1820 to 1840 the American Fur Company founded by him bought on the average 25,000 pounds of gunpowder a year from the du Ponts. Meanwhile, the mills imported 712,000 pounds of raw saltpeter a year from the East Indies and 94,000 pounds of sulphur from France and Italy. All told, since 1803 the enterprise had supplied 9,718,438 pounds of gunpowder, which led Eleuthère-Irénée to say: "Our establishment has already saved the Nation more than $2 million, which has been kept here in circulation instead of being taken out of the country to pay European industry, to which American industry is tributary."

When Lafayette was in America revisiting the battle-field of the Brandywine, he stopped at Eleutherian Mills. Before taking leave of his hosts, he wrote in the du Pont family album: "After having seen, near half a century ago, the banks of the Brandywine a scene of bloody fighting, I am happy now to find it the seat of industry, beauty and mutual friendship. July 25th, 1825, Lafayette."

In 1822 Eleuthère-Irénée received from President Monroe the coveted honor of appointment to the board of directors of the Bank of the United States, and under President John Quincy Adams he continued in this honorary post. Victor meanwhile came into his own in politics. Gifts united in the old Physiocrat had been divided up among the two children: Eleuthère-Irénée, drawn by science and progress, had become an industrialist, and Victor, the diplomat, man of the world and politician, had carved out a legislative career. Victor had at length lived up to his father's ideal of him as Pierre-Samuel expressed it once long ago. It was back in 1792 that the Physiocrat had written hopefully: "My son Victor was born with many qualities. Active, amiable, honest, very well endowed, with a just spirit, nonetheless he just missed ruining himself and probably would have, had not chance ruined all of us before him. He foolishly threw 40,000 francs out the window because I was of noble estate, a chevalier, councilor of state and collaborator of ministers of state. He thought it was beneath him to respect order and practice economy. Instead of making his own good reputation, he expected to profit by mine. But now I have faith that the loss of my fortune and my position . . . and his own native intelligence . . . have entirely corrected him."

Victor du Pont died suddenly in Philadelphia in 1827. He was only sixty years old. A year later it was Sophie's turn. Eleuthère-Irénée, during his last five years without Sophie, ceased to be the amazing businessman envied by his contemporaries. His colleagues often found him lost in long reveries at his work-table. Sometimes he talked about going to France. On October 31, 1834, he came to the same end as his older brother: he fell dead in a Philadelphia street. Perhaps he suffered a heart attack, or perhaps, as some thought, he was the victim of the cholera epidemic that had broken out some weeks earlier in Philadelphia. He was sixty-three years old.

5

The Community Society

Il faut une sorte d'esprit pour
faire fortune — et surtout une
grande fortune.
LA BRUYÈRE

NATURALLY ENOUGH it was Eleuthère-Irénée's oldest
son on whom fell the responsibility of taking his
father's place. Alfred Victor Philadelphe, thirty-six
years old in 1834, had grown up amid the din of pestles
grinding gunpowder in the mortars of the Eleutherian
Mills where, at twenty, his father had put him to work.
The only time he had spent away from home was his
two years studying chemistry at Dickinson College. His
father had tried to train him, but though he may have
been interested in this science, he seems to have had no
particular vocation for it. He was even less cut out for
managing his father's mill. It may be supposed that he
had inherited a taste for ideas from his physiocrat
grandfather much greater than any taste for business

from his father, and that he was in fact appalled at the thought of running the powder works.

Alfred Victor was born in Paris, his birth certificate tells us, "at 4 o'clock in the morning at 146 Rue de l'Oratoire, in the French Guards section, on the 24 Germinal in the year VI of the Republic." Unlike his younger brothers, he had spoken French before English; and it was working in French that he had helped his illustrious grandfather, Pierre-Samuel, compose one of his last works, *L'Instruction Publique en Amérique de Sud.* In delicate health, he had never worked steadily at the powder mill more than a couple of years at a time. When very young he had married the daughter of a French *émigré* by the name of La Motte, which had become Americanized into Lammot. The *National Encyclopedia of American Biography* says of him: "His life unfolded relatively without incident, but it was less the fault of the man, who was outstanding, than of his period, which was rather dull." Perhaps the best characterization of Eleuthère-Irénée's oldest son is as an enlightened but rather eclectic amateur. He would have been perfectly at home in a society of cultivated people, among whom he could have led a pleasant life living off his income. But he never felt at ease in the limited society into which chance had thrown him.

By dint of entreaty Alfred Victor's brother-in-law, Antoine Bidermann, husband of Evelina, was prevailed on to take over the reins of command for the time being

in Alfred's stead. He kept them until 1837, in which
year Antoine made up his mind to go with his wife and
son to live in Paris. However, while he served as regent
he did his job well; and when he left, after three years,
he turned back to Alfred Victor a going concern. All
the shares were now reunited in the Eleutherian Mills
strongbox, since Antoine Bidermann had relinquished
his personal interest in the business and had also bought
up for the family all shares belonging to outsiders. Thus,
the sole owners of the company were the children of its
founder Eleuthère-Irénée: the three sons Alfred Victor,
Henry, Alexis, and the four daughters Victorine, Evelina, Eleuthera, Sophie-Madeleine. Sophie married her
first cousin Samuel Francis, Victor's son and the future
admiral, thus bringing Victor's line for the first time
into the powder company's community partnership.

The result was that the du Ponts now lived and
worked in a closed community on the model of a religious order, or something like the disciples of Charles
Fourier, French founder of the socialist phalansteries,
who died in this same year, 1837. At last, the Eleuthère-
Irénée Du Pont Company was owner of all the family's
goods and chattels. To it belonged the houses and the
little plots of land enjoyed by the workers in the powder sheds. The company was owner, as well, of all the
houses in which members of the family lived. Each
house was allotted according to the number of children
in the household. Whenever a home was needed for

newlyweds and no house was available, the company built a new one.

Alfred Victor himself lived in one he had named Nemours, which his father had built for him at the time of his marriage in 1824. When he died in 1856, his widow kept on living in the house only until her son Lammot married. She then turned the place over to him and retired to a dwelling of more modest size, called Good Stay in memory of the house Bon Séjour where the family had first settled upon arriving in the United States.

When Antoine Bidermann restored the management to the unwilling Alfred Victor, the latter, as the eldest, had the power of signature for the company, to sign drafts, receipts and orders. It was he, too, who officially occupied the position of company director. However, he had insisted that his two brothers Henry and Alexis also share this title, and that all company profits should be divided equally seven ways. It seems that when Bidermann departed, he turned over his share, but not his wife Evelina's.

No one was paid a salary; each drew on cash according to his needs, keeping a record to turn in at the year's end. As an example of this sharing, even the horses and carriages belonged to the Eleuthère-Irénée Du Pont Company. In the Longwood Archives is the following note from Alfred Victor to Henry:

December 27th, 1850

My brother,

I must go to Phil. before the 31. I have been putting it off for nearly 3 weeks. My object is to pay off every small debt I owe. To do this, I wish you send me a check on Phil. Bank for $100 and I shall draw $400 out of Union Bk.

Your brother
ALFRED V.

I should wish to have the carriage at 11 o'clock, for Meta must go with me; otherwise the [*illegible*] would answer.

Alfred Victor had resigned from his duties several years before he wrote this note. His poor health had served as a pretext for unburdening himself of his responsibilities and asking his brother Henry to take his place. It might perhaps have been more logical if Alfred Victor had been succeeded by his oldest son, rather than his brother; but this son, Eleuthère-Irénée, II, was only twenty years old and lacked experience.

In 1846, while Alfred Victor was still in power, the company had found itself involved in a second war. This time, however, the United States was not as in 1812 the attacked nation but the aggressor, the victim being Mexico. It has been asserted that Pierre-Samuel du Pont in 1802 adjured President Jefferson to warn his countrymen against the temptation of self-aggrandizement at the expense of their weak neighbor. President James Polk, goaded by an impatient public,

The Accolade

ainting done in 1944, representing the Physiocrat Pierre-Samuel du Pont with
his sons Eleuthère-Irénée, center, and Victor, at right

Ile St. Louis, Paris, 1961.
Entrance to the old du Pont printing house, at right

DIXIE REYNOLDS

Four generations of du Ponts: Pierre S., III, Pierre S., IV, and Pierre S., V,
under a portrait of the first Pierre-Samuel du Pont

The village of Chevannes, near Nemours, France, home town of the du Ponts
before they moved to the U. S. A.

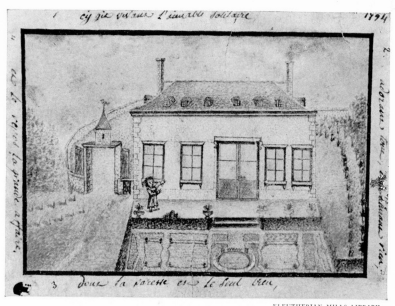

A 1794 sketch of Bois des Fossés, near Chevannes, France.
The du Ponts lived here from 1774 to 1799

The lane leading to Bois des Fossés, France, as it is today

The port of La Rochelle, France, circa 1800.
The du Ponts sailed from here in 1799

The coat of arms used
by the du Pont family

The authentic du Pont coat of arms
as described in *Le Grand Armorial
de France*, with *Rectitudine Sto* to
be placed above the shield

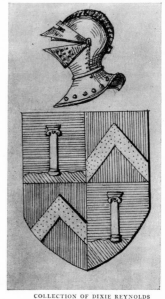

DIXIE REYNO

A 1961 view of Nemours, France.
Pierre-Samuel du Pont, elected Deputy from Nemours in 1789,
added "de Nemours" to his name to identify himself

Victor du Pont, Virginia farmer, at his mother's home in 1960

In 1805, Victor du Pont was junior warden of a Masonic lodge
in New York

Nineteenth-century gunpowder advertisement

A textile trademark of Du Pont in 1810. At right, Don Pedro

A statue of the fertile ram, Don Pedro, in a du Pont garden

Miss Aileen du Pont, family guardian of French traditions, 1960

The graves of Alfred I. du Pont and his dog Yip lie under this imposing bell tow
on his estate, Nemours

Architect Alfred Victor, in 1948. Only son of Alfred I. du Pont

DIXIE REYNOLDS

A 1961 du Pont bride — Nancy Christina — in a 1929 Du Pont automobile

yielded to this temptation. The role of the United States, Polk said, had been clearly laid down for them by "manifest destiny," in pushing them ever toward the West to settle on Pacific shores. From Mexico the United States demanded, and got, not only all of California and Texas, but also the abrogation by Mexico of all rights to Utah, Colorado and New Mexico. Total American combat losses in this enormously profitable operation were fortunately only 1753 killed and 4000 wounded. The operation was also highly profitable for the Du Pont Company. The administration had bought from them — and for it paid a handsome price — a million pounds of gunpowder. Thanks to the war, Du Pont business had increased to a point where in 1849 they produced 400,000 pounds of powder more than in the previous record year of 1848!

Henry was very different from his older brother. In the first place, he was completely American, born and reared in the United States. Where Alfred Victor had no liking for command, Henry certainly did, no mistake about it. His boyhood ambition had been to become an Army officer, and he was graduated from West Point. On his father's death, when Henry was twenty-two, he resigned from the Army to go to work with his two brothers at Eleutherian Mills. Alexis was only eighteen when at this time he left college to go to work.

Judging Henry in the light of his love for the military,

it seems hardly possible that he had any liking for the system of community capitalism so strictly applied by his older brother from 1837 to 1850. And it is surprising that this régime of collective responsibility — or irresponsibility — had not produced disastrous results, especially during a period such as this, when a succession of economic crises born of the Industrial Revolution swept both America and Europe.

In any case, it did not take the personnel of the Du Pont Company long to find out that in Henry they had a real head man. Nor did it take Henry du Pont long to discover that company finances were on the anemic side. Slight in build, he invariably wore a frock coat of severe cut and a stovepipe hat, perhaps because he thought this outfit made him look taller. With his red chin-whiskers and shaven lips he was the image of the caricature of "Uncle Sam," the image known by the Europeans of that era, such as the young Queen Victoria, the prince-president Louis Napoleon and a certain obscure German socialist named Karl Marx.

In 1846 Henry was named adjutant general of the Delaware Militia and, in 1861, major-general commanding Delaware's Volunteers. Everybody called him General. Smoking expensive Havana cigars was the only luxury this extremely frugal man ever permitted himself. Thriftily and authoritatively rejecting all everyday innovations, which seemed to him to be nothing but useless expense, he refused even to change the furniture in the tiny office his father and older brother had used before him. It was in this room, a few steps away from his home, that he settled down in 1850. And here he worked to the end of his "reign," that is, up to the time of his death thirty-nine years later in 1889. He never allowed gaslight to be installed, nor even electricity, despite all attempts to modernize the office made by his nephew Alfred, who had come into the company. On his desk he had three candles. He took care that they burned to the end.

It was only during the last years of his life that he permitted a typewriter to be introduced into his offices, and then only as a result of a ruse. His secretary Frank Haley, without telling the General, bought a machine and practiced on it at home. When he felt he was able to type passably well, he took a long chance and typed out a final version of the rough drafts of letters which the General had given him as usual the night before. Concealing his astonishment, General Henry read the correspondence spread out in front of him in this improved form. Before going to lunch he simply said to Haley that he could continue with his typewriting and that the company would bear the cost of the machine.

One of the first moves the General made in 1850 was to call the two principal partners to his office: his brother Alexis and Alfred Victor's young son Eleuthère-Irénée, II, who were in charge of gunpowder manufacture. He explained to them that America was entering new times, in which Du Pont would be faced by competitors who would be outstripping the company before long if they were allowed to get away with it. It seems that in upholding its reputation, Du Pont was turning out nothing but high-quality products, while their competitors offered their customers poorer quality powders at a much cheaper price. And these powders were good enough for blasting in the West or coal mining in Pennsylvania. The General said: "I am asking you to study how to make powder comparable to theirs. When this has been done, I will personally send agents as far as California to sell it."

Once this plan was adopted, Alexis had no trouble presenting the General, several weeks later, with specimens of cheap gunpowder such as he had asked for. The General himself, putting on his stovepipe hat, took these samples to his principal competitors, and we can imagine him declaring stoutly in army style something like this: "We can manufacture the same products as you and at the same price as you. If you insist, there will be a price war between us, and we all will be ruined. If you want to behave like reasonable people, let's get this thing straightened out. For my part I'm ready to sign an 'economic arrangement' with you, fixing our prices at a level that will leave all of us an adequate margin of profit. How do you feel about it?" Everyone signed the proposed agreement. The question was settled. In a short time the Du Pont Company was prospering again, furnishing gunpowder for the Franco-British fleets and the Allied expeditionary corps which fought in the Crimea (1854-1855) against the Russians. The du Pont fortune grew.

Thanks to the huge profits realized from these foreign orders, the company was in a solid financial position during the critical year of 1857 and able easily to survive when so many other companies went on the rocks.

The fact that the great European nations should have thought to call on Du Pont for their powder would seem to indicate that the reputation of the Wilmington works had spread beyond the boundaries of the United States. What a change since 1842, at which time Alcide d'Orbigny, a traveler from La Rochelle, wrote about the Brandywine: "Its gristmills are the largest in the U.S.A. with the exception of those in Rochester." He made no mention of the industry founded by his fellow-countryman du Pont!

The truth is that even as late as 1896 there was no concept in France of the importance of this enterprise. In the first complete edition of Chateaubriand's *Mémoires d'Outre-Tombe* published that year by Garnier, there is only this simple reference to the du Ponts: "The two sons of du Pont run an important agricultural development in America."

Family tradition has made a great man of General Henry. Without deflating this image, it must be admitted that this dictatorial man with a talent for old-fashioned action understood nothing or very little of scientific progress, a serious lack indeed in his business. The idea of substituting sodium nitrate for saltpeter in the manufacture of gunpowder had long been known, but at Du Pont the techniques of the past lingered on.

Fortunately, one member of the family did have a talent for chemistry and an open mind toward innovation: Lammot du Pont, Alfred Victor's second son. Born in 1831, he was not yet thirty when he was sent to Europe, like his grandfather in earlier years to Essonnes, to inform himself of technical progress on the Continent. He had graduated from the University of Pennsylvania and had studied the new European discoveries, and in 1857 he invented a powder-making process that called for mixing 72 parts of nitrate of Peru (sodium nitrate) with 16 parts of charcoal and 12 of refined sulphur. The product of this mixture he called Powder B or "soda powder." Tests in the Pennsylvania mines showed that the new product had an explosive power superior to that of black powder. Immediately it was in great demand, so much so that the powder sheds of the Eleutherian Mills were unable to fill all the orders. When the rival establishment of Parrish, Silver and Co. was for sale in Pennsylvania, the General quickly acquired the property and Lammot modernized it for the manufacture of Powder B at the rate of 36,000 tons a year. It was Du Pont's first branch outside Delaware. It was, too, the first time that the Du Pont Company was producing strictly industrial explosive.

In 1857, Alexis, the General's young brother and the company's technical director, was killed in an explosion, and Lammot took his place. From the start Lammot had the title of partner, as had been the case with his older brother, Eleuthère-Irénée, II. Upon Lammot's return from Europe in 1858 he made further good use of his new technical information by teaming up with Thomas J. Rodman, inventor of the giant cannon that bore his name. It was at this time that the Eleuthère-Irénée Du Pont Company began to manufacture special large-grained powder for heavy-caliber artillery pieces — the guns that the Yankees were to be the first to use in the war against the South.

Any number of books have been written on the painful conflict between the Northern and the Southern States, and they invariably point out the general technical superiority and industrial power of the North. They usually fail, however, to give due emphasis to the day the frontier state of Delaware went over to the Yankee side instead of falling in with the South as might easily have been the case. Indeed, in 1861 the Confederates had at their disposal only two very small powder works, barely sufficient to meet the needs of their troops, one at Nashville, another in South Carolina. Not until 1862 were they able to set up a third in Georgia, which was the only company to make Powder B for them. How different history's course might have been if the state where the du Ponts were located had come out for the Secessionists. In this broad connection a detail is worth mentioning: Bauduy P. Garesché, grandson of the Bauduy who was a Du Pont partner at the time the Brandywine powder mills were founded, joined the Confederates. He had learned how to manufacture powder with his father, when his father had started a powder mill at Eden Park in competition with Du Pont. As a colonel, he was put in charge of the Confederate Powder Service, which set up the South Carolina mill. In *The Life of Col. Julius P. Garesché* there is the following anecdote. General Grant, in camp near Richmond, is supposed to have said to one of his friends: "I wish I could catch that Bauduy Garesché. . . . Oh, I would not harm a hair on his head, but if I caught him I would keep him close, and not exchange him for 10,000 men. The powder he manufactures for the South is far superior to ours. . . ." The author of this work was the son of Colonel Julius Garesché. One wonders if this anecdote was invented out of filial devotion or resentment toward the du Ponts. Or was it true?

In 1860, General Henry had voted and worked for John Bell rather than Lincoln. The General believed that with Bell it would be possible to avoid civil war. On the other hand, immediately after the fall of Fort

Sumter, when the moment of decision was at hand, he informed his Virginia agent, who had just forwarded a big order, that he must regretfully refuse to fill it if Virginia declared for the Confederacy. Shortly afterward he let Lincoln know that he could count on the fullest cooperation of Du Pont in supplying the Union armies.

General Henry's own family was not to be spared the conflict of conscience which harrowed so many Americans. Eleuthère-Irénée, II, had married Miss Charlotte Henderson of Virginia. His mother, however, although born in France, was so radically pro-Lincoln that the two women lived in a state of chronic hostility. Forced to make a choice, Alfred Victor's oldest son had a falling out with his mother. He did not even go to see her on her deathbed.

General Henry, though commander of the Delaware Volunteers, took no part in any military action; but his oldest son, Henry Algernon, just out of West Point, distinguished himself, it appears, with his artillery regiment. His cousin Samuel Francis, Victor's son, a Navy captain at the start of hostilities, was given the mission of blockading Southern ports, and carried it out so well that his vessels were able to prevent both the departure of boats carrying cargoes of cotton and the entry of ships with arms and ammunition. Congress honored him by making him rear admiral, a rank created on the occasion of his promotion in 1862. One of the busiest intersections in Washington today is Du Pont Circle, named in honor of Admiral Samuel Francis du Pont.

All through the War between the States a permanent guard was set up in the Brandywine area to prevent sabotage. According to one estimate, Du Pont supplied the Union with between 3.5 and 4 million pounds of powder, including a certain amount of the Mammoth Powder deriving from tests made by Lammot, which provided naval guns with a range unknown up to that time. Its effectiveness became evident when, on March 9, 1862, the Union ironclad *Monitor* defeated the Confederate *Merrimac*, which created such a sensation that *The Times* of London was moved to write: "We had 149 vessels of the first class. Now we have only two." After 1862 England and France, by and large, built only iron vessels. The end of the wooden ship had come. The *Monitor's* victory also signaled the coming of big guns of long range using as propellants the large "grains" of powder such as Du Pont's Mammoth Powder.

In 1875 Europeans experimented with giant guns loaded with 100 to 180 pounds of black powder. The Italians armed their heavy cruiser *Duilio* with guns weighing a hundred tons, made for them by Armstrong in England, and firing an 850-pound projectile a distance of eight miles. In 1876 the English on their own account armed the *Invincible* with 81-ton cannon comparable in power to those on the *Duilio*. And in Germany, Krupp came out with a cannon called the "Kolossal," weighing 200 tons.

The du Ponts certainly were keeping an eye on these new European developments. Among them was one particularly interesting Russian invention, presented by the engineer Popof, called "the floating saucer." It was a circular boat protected by 18-inch armorplate and armed with six 41-ton cannon placed in a central turret. Designed for the defense of Black Sea ports, this floating saucer could turn so as to fire all guns at once in the direction of the enemy.

It is difficult today to estimate the profits the du Ponts made from the war, for it seems to be strictly accurate, as always contended by General Henry, that what they gained by selling to the government they lost in great measure by not being able at the same time to sell to private customers.

Completely engrossed as they were in war production, it is quite true that they were forced to neglect their customers in the West just at a time when their numbers were increasing; and a rival firm, the California Powder Works, stepped in to profit from this situation. A lot of time and effort was needed to regain Du Pont's position in this new market, once it had been lost to another company. Not long after the Civil War, Adams & Bishop's *Transcontinental Guide* mentioned that powder was "the railroad companies' greatest source of expense. Before the war they were paying $2.25 a barrel for it. Afterwards it rose to $5. . . ."

In 1845 a Swiss, Frederick Schoenbein, had invented guncotton (cellulose nitrate), and an Italian, Ascanio Sobrero, nitroglycerin. General Henry had paid no particular attention to these inventions, but Lammot had immediately realized their importance. His Uncle Henry was primarily concerned with the accidents being caused by these new explosives, since the newspapers had been playing up the tragedies. Not so the progressive Lammot. He foresaw that the manufacturing process would be perfected. And this is exactly what was done by Nobel in 1862 when he used *Kieselguhr*, or diatomaceous earth, to absorb the nitroglycerin, thus converting the dangerously explosive liquid into a more stable solid. Progress along this line became even more striking when Nobel, a little later on, got the idea of using mercuric fulminate to detonate the nitroglycerin. After 1865, plants for the manufacture of nitroglycerin, or "blasting oil," were built first in Germany and Sweden, then in all European countries, but Henry du Pont, largest explosives manufacturer in the United States, still refused to be convinced.

Meanwhile the American press played up to the hilt two tragic accidents with nitroglycerin: the first involving the steamship *Europa*, which blew up in the

port of Colón in 1866, killing sixty-six persons and caus-
ing a million dollars' damages; the second an accident
in San Francisco which claimed fourteen victims. An
aroused Congress prohibited the transport and sale of
nitroglycerin in America, which was all to the good, as
can be imagined, for Du Pont business. But neither
parliamentary assemblies nor outraged tycoons can stop
progress, and thanks to Nobel, progress continued. In
1866 dynamite — nitroglycerin stabilized by a mixture
of ground brick — was invented. Would General Henry
never see the light?

The General's strong point, basically, was his ability
to organize business combines. In this period his only
thought was to rig the market by making deals with
competitors as he had done before in 1850. There were
only two competitors capable of giving him any trouble:
Laflin & Rand Powder and Hazard Powder Company.
Like Du Pont, they made only "conventional" powders,
leaving it to outside adventurers to engage in the clan-
destine manufacture of high explosives in imitation of
European products. In April, 1872, General Henry
called a meeting of his colleagues at his New York office at 70 Wall Street. There an agreement was signed
by the Big Three and some firms of lesser importance,
bringing into being the Gunpowder Trade Association
or Powder Trust. This Association not only required its
members all to sell at the same price, but also divided
up the country into exclusive sales territories.

Finally, in 1876, Congress apparently having forgotten its strictures of 1866, dynamite was put to public test for the first time in America — but not thanks to Du Pont. On September 24 a huge crowd gathered on the banks of the East River to watch a prodigious spectacle: 40 tons of dynamite (13,596 sticks) had been placed under the rock reefs of Hell Gate which impeded entry via the river to the port of New York. The explosive charges were all linked together and to a central point by 28 miles of electric wire. At the moment designated by the organizers of the ceremony, a little two-and-a-half-year-old girl — not a du Pont, alas, but the daughter of a General Newton who had believed in the future of Nobel's work — pressed a button and a tremendous explosion blew up the reefs. Lammot's chagrin as he watched this perfectly successful experiment can easily be imagined.

This same year Lammot advised the General to buy the California Powder Company and the General took his advice. Since 1863 this company had been trying to manufacture, under the name of "Black Hercules," a hybrid product consisting of black powder and nitroglycerin mixed, a concoction which, however, had never given satisfactory results. Later, around 1870, James Howden, a San Francisco chemist, inspired by Nobel's discoveries, had taken out a patent based on this combination. He used a formula in which 75 per cent nitroglycerin was absorbed by a mixture of magnesium carbonate and potassium nitrate and gave to his product the name "White Hercules." California Powder bought up the patent. Nobel then brought an action against Howden for patent infringement, but it was dismissed by an American court. At this time America offered foreign inventors the least protection of all the big nations, that is to say, almost none. (Many Europeans think this still holds true.)

When General Henry bought this company a couple of years later it was manufacturing, under the trade name of "White Hercules," the imitation of Nobel's dynamite invented by Howden. Thus General Henry got control of a firm making one of the high explosives he had refused to produce in the Du Pont works. . . . Lammot had won.

In 1876 Hazard Powder began to experience difficulties, and without saying a word to anyone the General bought it for a song. An even greater advantage accruing from the deal involved representation on the Gunpowder Association's board of directors. Du Pont de Nemours, Laflin & Rand, and Hazard each had 10 votes, Oriental Powder 6, and Austin American and Miami 4 apiece, making a total of 44 votes. The moment General Henry secretly acquired Hazard Powder, Du Pont was certain of 20 votes — an assured controlling bloc.

The du Ponts now held a powerful position in both

East and West. Only the South remained, where normal activity was now coming to life. By a master stroke the General got his hands on the Sycamore Mills, whereupon that company's New Orleans sales offices became his. Finally, from 1876 to 1880 ten other companies came under Du Pont control. In 1881 Laflin & Rand was the only independent of any size still surviving. Remarkably, General Henry had at no time contracted debts in forming his combines. The firm owed not a cent. Investment capital had been supplied solely by the family from reserves accumulated from the profits of their flourishing capitalist enterprise, the partners of which, even now in 1880, were still using the community-ownership system started by Alfred Victor in 1837.

However, this community-ownership system of the Eleuthère-Irénée Du Pont Company was no longer governed by a family assembly, including women, as in the time of the indifferent Alfred Victor, but was dominated now by the autocratic General Henry.

He was stubborn and did not like advice, but it would be misleading to conclude that Henry never listened. He had the good sense, as we have seen, to buy the California Company on his nephew Lammot's suggestion, so as to regain the business in the West lost while supplying the Civil War needs. And it was Lammot again to whom he confessed that since the sale of high explosives manufactured by California Powder under Du Pont control was very profitable, it might be to the company's interest to make them in the East as well. His personal fear of dynamite, nitroglycerin and such products was one thing, but business was another.

Lammot had taken a roundabout way to persuade his uncle to this policy. As a Du Pont delegate to the Gunpowder Association, he had become friendly with Solomon Turck, president of Laflin & Rand. At a meeting of the Association's board, better known under the name of the Powder Trust, he persuaded Solomon Turck that since the dynamite business had a promising future, the two of them ought to form a partnership so as to make the most of it. Turck took to the proposal and later submitted a scheme along this line to the General.

In 1880 a new company was formed with a capitalization of $300,000, with equal participation by Du Pont, Laflin & Rand, and Hazard. (Apparently Turck was unaware that Du Pont in fact controlled Hazard.) A powder works was built near Gibbston, New Jersey, across from Wilmington on the farther bank of the Delaware River at the confluence of the Repaupo. For reasons of euphony Repauno replaced Repaupo, and the new enterprise was registered under the name of Repauno Chemicals, Inc. Nobel would not be able to draw a cent of royalties from these manufacturers, since the formula patented by Howden and already exploited by the Du Pont affiliate in California would be used. This formula was to be modified, moreover, as Lammot had intended, by substituting wood pulp for sugar, and the product would be sold in the East under the Atlas trademark. Lammot du Pont, it went without saying, was to manage Repauno Chemicals. He, meanwhile, had diplomatically insisted on having as his second-in-command the General's youngest son, William. Up until now, William's job has been to supervise the development of the extensive du Pont land holdings, by farming them or putting the land to use as pasturage for Merino sheep.

Lammot's diplomacy was paying off. The sale of dynamite in the East, and even more in the West, increased at a dizzy rate. But the California Powder Company was having trouble supervising, from a distance, production in one of its explosive mills in Cleveland. The General came forward with a new arrangement, imposing the following terms: By agreement with Solomon Turck, the General would merge the Cleveland mill with Repauno, and their activities would be unified under the firm name of Hercules Powder Company. Shortly afterwards, Lammot and Turck secretly bought for their personal account a majority interest in the Giant Powder Company, a New Jersey firm manufacturing fulminate detonators for dynamite, as well as a "gelatin explosive" under a Nobel license. Thus, without arousing notice, Lammot and his colleague came into possession of the right henceforward to use Nobel patents. All that remained was to "organize" the market and price of high explosives in the United States as had been done for gunpowder. The dynamite cartel had been launched.

We can only speculate on how Lammot's bold initiative and the way he had taken personal control of Giant Powder sat with the General. All that is known for a certainty is that Lammot left Delaware to open up an office in Philadelphia, and that as early as 1880, claiming preoccupation with Repauno, he resigned from the Du Pont de Nemours board of directors. But he was not to profit very long from his double success as businessman and high-caliber technician. In 1884 he was killed in an explosion at Repauno which also took the lives of three of his collaborators. Ironically, it was Lammot who had had no fear of the high explosives. The General lost no time in letting Lammot's widow know that since the oldest of her sons, Pierre, was only fourteen her duty was to accept a plan which to the General's way of thinking would "straighten everything out." The Du Pont Company would buy back from Lammot's widow all of Lammot's shares both in Hercules and in the Giant Powder Company.

William, the General's son, was subsequently made president of Hercules Powder Company. Lammot's old office in Philadelphia, where William had been his assistant, was immediately closed. Thus Lammot's heritage was regulated in the best interests of the company and of the family as a whole.

However, after General Henry's death, four years later, the succession was going to be complicated.

6

The End of the Community Society

THE GENERAL DIED in August, 1889, after a brief ill-
ness. The powerful entrepreneur who had made
the Du Pont Company into one of the great industrial
organizations of America faded out of the picture at
the age of seventy-seven, without, it might be said,
ever having wasted a moment's thought on his mor-
tality. Pascal speaks of those men who "not having
been able to conquer death . . . make up their minds
. . . never to think about it." It seems an inherent
weakness in empire-builders, dictators and other such
people whose strength appears formidable that they
are in fact not sure enough of themselves to train their
successors.

The oldest of the General's two sons, Henry Algernon,
a former Army officer who had left the service with the
rank of colonel, was anything but inclined to live in the
General's shadow. He had carved out a highly satisfactory niche for himself by becoming president of the
Wilmington and Northern Railroad Company. He was

completely out of touch with Du Pont affairs. The second son, William, the family did not consider capable of governing the empire.

Other than these, the most logical candidates to succeed the General were not in Henry's line, but rather in his late brother Alfred Victor's line. When Alfred Victor retired he had yielded his place to brother Henry, but this was only because his children were young. It was now Alfred Victor's grandson Alfred I., twenty-five years old in 1889, who could claim the most qualifications for the top of the pyramid — the same Alfred who as a boy had fiercely defended his brothers' and sisters' right to defy company authority and remain in their home, Swamp Hall, after they were orphaned.

But for a variety of reasons — which we shall go into later on — the family preferred to ignore Alfred Victor's line and to turn to the line of Alexis, the General's youngest brother, who had been killed in an explosion. To this branch belonged Eugene, married to his cousin Amelia, a man of forty-nine, a chemist who had made his career in the Du Pont Company. Industrious, serious, sparing of words, he was the self-effacing sort of person who had been able to get along with his Uncle Henry. At the same time, it was said, he was by no means lacking in executive ability, and was a conscientious technician. In any case, it was he whom the family chose to direct the company.

No sooner had he taken over his new duties than Eugene made a big decision. On land belonging to Du Pont de Nemours he ordered the construction of a new building, to be lighted by electricity and provided with a telephone. As soon as this modest building was finished, the touchingly small office that had been good enough for the General was abandoned. Still other novelties were to mark the period of transition into which the company was entering.

First of all, there was the question of William. Chagrined at having been left standing in the wings, the General's son played into the hands of critics by getting mixed up in scandals. He got divorced, the first of all the du Ponts to do so, and thereby created a thoroughly troublesome precedent. The woman whom he divorced, his cousin Mary L. du Pont, married the lawyer who had handled her side of the case, and William himself remarried someone deemed "unacceptable" by the family. William's divorce precipitated the first serious du Pont family crisis. True, in 1865 the marriage of the brilliant chemist Lammot had been disapproved by some of his relatives because the girl he wed, Mary Belin, was the daughter of one of his father's bookkeepers and of Jewish extraction to boot. But the quarrel had been quickly appeased by General Henry after he, whose decisions were never questioned, had openly taken Lammot and Mary's side.

But this time the General was dead, and it is doubtful in any event whether he would have approved his son's divorce and remarriage.

Eugene was commissioned to tell the reprobate that he would do everybody a big favor by going somewhere else to live. William bowed to the family verdict. He resigned all his posts and went away, first to Paris, then later to Virginia, where, it is said, he settled down. One of the jobs thus vacated, that of manager of Repauno, was given to a newcomer, J. Amory Haskell, who had enjoyed excellent business relations with Du Pont while managing a coal-mining business and who was highly recommended by Laflin and Rand, co-owners of Repauno. Haskell, only thirty-one years old, brought with him as assistant Hamilton Barksdale, also thirty-one. Neither of them was a chemist or a powder man, but both were astute businessmen.

But the essential issue remained: who was to get the title of partner in the Du Pont Company, abandoned by William? Alfred I. boldly asserted his right to this partnership. Eugene, who disliked Alfred, had up till now conceded him only a miserly percentage of the company profits, and now resisted on this point. But Alfred insisted. When all was settled, in 1892, Eugene was obliged to part with William's share and give it half to Alfred and half to Charles I. du Pont, who was a great-grandson of Victor. Alfred had succeeded in getting his foot inside the door. But he was not able to overcome the prejudices of the other members of the board. When he attended board meetings they acted as if he were not there.

It appears that Alfred I. some years earlier had got himself in the bad graces of the very relatives whose partner he now wished to become by failing in the mission they had assigned him of ferreting out French government trade secrets in the manufacture of smokeless powder. This powder had been made in French government powder plants since 1885 according to Vieille's patent. It was known that the product was based on pyronitrocellulose, the same substance which in 1870 had served an American, J. W. Hyatt, as point of departure in his invention of celluloid. The United States government was anxious to have this smokeless powder made in the United States. To this end, the government in 1889 turned to Du Pont, but the company at the time was unable to deliver the goods. There followed Alfred's mission; but it was suspected in Paris what he was up to, and he found all doors closed. As a last desperate measure he went to London and Brussels. But he was young and probably naïve. A Belgian firm, Coopal et Cie, sold him, at a fancy price, not only a manufacturing license for a process which they claimed was superior to the French one, but also machinery which they said was indispensable. Eugene immediately got the impression that his envoy had been taken in. He was certain of it when the new powder was tested. He never forgave Alfred this costly blunder.

Later, the Du Pont laboratories at Carney Point developed a process for the manufacture of a smokeless powder to be used for hunting, which had come into wide use after 1893. At last, the purchase of a German patent from the Vereinigte Koeln-Rottweiler Pulverfabrik enabled Du Pont to make a military smokeless powder of suitable quality. But even this success did not soften Eugene's anger at Alfred's failure.

It was all the more urgent right now for the American government to have smokeless powder manufactured, since in 1892 it had adopted for Army use the Krag Jorgensen rifle, designed in Norway, and this new rifle could not use black powder cartridges. In 1898 when the war with Spain* broke out, the company, no longer having to fear foreign competition, for the time being concentrated all its resources on making powder and explosives for the United States government.

In the roads of Manila, thanks to Du Pont propellants, all that Commodore Dewey had to do was stay

* In 1896 the Aetna Powder Co., member of the dynamite cartel, had sent a shipment of dynamite to South Africa. The English, who customarily supplied this region, took a dim view of this. Nobel Explosives Ltd., and Rheinische-Westphaler of Cologne moved together in a counterattack. The Nobel group, to which they were subsidiary, bought a large tract near Jamesburg, N.J., announcing that the Anglo-German group intended to build a dynamite plant there for the United States market. Messrs. Barksdale of Repauno and Fay of Aetna jumped aboard the first liner leaving for London on May 18, 1897. Eugene followed shortly after and a peace treaty was signed by the companies exactly delimiting their world sales territories.

out of range and shoot at will at the old and defenseless Spanish vessels. As for the du Ponts, they could thank their lucky stars for having bought, in 1897, from the American inventor Hudson Maxim, his patent for the manufacture of smokeless powder. Maxim had turned his invention over to Eugene du Pont for a guaranteed payment of $400 a month for seventeen years.

Du Pont was given a contract to supply the government with 5 million pounds of powder. From May to September, 1898 — the armistice was signed in the fall and the Treaty of Paris in December — they had delivered 2.5 million pounds. Though the company certainly made money out of the war, it must be said that Eugene drove himself all out to see that the goods were delivered with the greatest possible dispatch.

Eugene's health gave cause for alarm. He fell gravely ill at the same time that it became evident that the financial structure of the Du Pont enterprise was not keeping up with their expansion.

On the recommendation of Colonel Henry Algernon du Pont, the family partnership begun in 1837 was finally dissolved. The company was incorporated in the state of Delaware as E. I. du Pont de Nemours & Co., on October 23, 1899, one hundred years after the family arrived in Newport.

Taking everything into consideration, one might say that Eugene's directorship was lackluster, but not inept. In the new company which had just been formed and incorporated, he kept the title of president. Vice-presidencies were given to two old gentlemen in poor health, Dr. Alexis du Pont and Francis G. du Pont, brothers of Eugene. Their father was Alexis I., youngest son of the founder. Charles I. du Pont, young but sickly, was promised the post of secretary-treasurer. Alfred, used to being held at arm's length, had to be satisfied with the title of director without actually being a member of the board. This state of affairs lasted until the death of Eugene in January, 1902.

In the field of labor relations, too, changes had to be made. The firm was no longer getting along well with its workers as it had nearly always in the past. From 1870 to 1890 some 15 million immigrants had arrived in America, among them many Irish fleeing the frightful misery of their homeland, turbulent Sicilians, and Chinese landing in masses on the Pacific Coast. A great tide of Negroes flooded north toward the industrial states after the liberation of the slaves. How could this influx of a generally inferior labor force fail to incite American management to pay its workers poor wages? After 1869 a movement grew into being — the Knights of Labor — which tried to unite the workers into making a common front against abuses, and which, after 1885, grew immensely and moved into action. It unleashed strikes, some of them bloody, in a number of industrial centers where working conditions were particularly shocking. All this development was correctly interpreted by a future President of the United States, Theodore Roosevelt, when he wrote: "The former intimate relations between employer and employee have disappeared. Before, both of them knew each other well, their relations were human. But magnates who employ thousands of workers can no longer have such relations."

In the little city of Wilmington, only vague echoes were heard of the troubles that had broken out elsewhere. As long as General Henry was on hand, thanks to the company old-timers his humanitarian paternalism had worked. However, as the business grew, the firm had to hire new personnel, especially at Repauno. The younger people, coming from areas where agitators had successfully operated, were opposed to this paternalism.

Fortunately for E. I. du Pont de Nemours & Co., the athletic young Haskell, who had just been taken into the clan, had had dealings with strikers in the Pennsylvania coal mines, where a secret society known as the Molly Maguires for a time had terrorized the workers. He knew how to handle the workers' demands; and thanks to him, labor difficulties at Du Pont were apparently reduced to a minimum. Nevertheless, two fires suspected of being of incendiary origin broke out on du Pont family property, and sabotage was also suspected in an explosion of 200 tons of cannon powder at one of the mills in October, 1889.

It is and it has been the policy of the Du Pont Company that no employee need be a member of any labor union. In fact, less than 8 per cent of them are cardholders of national Unions but over 65 per cent of wage-roll employees are represented by independent unions and 18 per cent are not unionized at all. The wages paid by the Du Pont Company to their workers are, according to the labor relations office of the company, generally the highest paid locally for comparable work, but they are not uniform in every plant and in every state. In the contracts signed by the national Unions, the salaries are uniform and recently the AFL-CIO union leaders have been insisting more on fringe benefits than on higher salaries for their members. It seems that the social benefits accorded to their workers by Du Pont are rather large. Du Pont's pension plan, originated in 1904, was one of the first in U.S. industry. At no cost to the employees, it provides an automatic pension to the worker who reaches 65 after 15 years of service. Other employee relations plans cover disability wages, vacations, salary allotment insurance, and so on. Since 1939, total man-days lost by work stoppages in Du Pont's regular manufacturing operations represented .03 per cent of man-days. The average for the same period has been .34 per cent for all industry in the U.S. "*Et nunc erudimini,*" as my son's Latin teacher would say.

7

The Triumvirs

> Discerning critics have looked
> upon romance as history that
> could have been and upon
> history as romance that came
> true.
>
> ANDRÉ GIDE
> *Les Caves du Vatican*

IN 1902 when Eugene died, Colonel Henry Algernon du Pont, the General's oldest son, in the position of *chef de famille*, was less interested than ever in devoting his time to the company. In the first place, he liked very much being president of his railroad company; and beyond that, he had his mind set on getting elected senator from Delaware — in which he succeeded, in 1906. The other two Du Pont vice-presidents were not in good health. And the last member of the family council, Charles I., was even more valetudinarian and in fact shortly followed Eugene into the grave.

Only one possibility seemed left — Alfred I. — but the

family did not want him. Driven to desperation by this impasse, the family, for the first time in the company's history, considered a stranger, Hamilton Barksdale — though actually he was not so much of an outsider, since he had married Ethel du Pont, Charles I.'s sister. A civil engineer, graduate of the University of Virginia, brilliant assistant of J. Amory Haskell, Barksdale would have been technically qualified to succeed Eugene du Pont, but he declined the offer. One solution was left: sell the business. Francis G. called a shareholders' meeting, all present being members of the family, to propose that the company be sold to Laflin & Rand, the only competitor of consequence, for 12 million dollars. The price was agreeable to the other party and Francis G. felt it was a reasonable deal.

His words fell into a heavy silence. Alfred I., who had come straight from the plant in working clothes, with his cyclist's pants and his powder-blackened hands, Alfred, the one from whom everybody expected a scene, like the rest uttered not a word. The motion went to a vote, and the proposal to sell the company was on the verge of being adopted when Alfred leaped to his feet, rushed to the door, put his back to it, and yelled: "I'll buy the business!" "As you can imagine," he said later on, "this announcement caused some consternation and a good deal of surprise. . . . Mr. Francis G. objected that I was in no position to buy the company. . . . 'And why not?' I asked him. . . . I reminded him that, on the contrary, by virtue of inheritance, I had every right to do so. I added that my money was surely as good as anyone else's. I asked only one week to raise the desired sum."

Alfred's brief version does not completely tally with what other witnesses say. Their description of this extraordinary scene has an entirely different emphasis: Cousin Alfred crying out in a too-shrill voice, Uncle Francis G. cold and suspicious, the family all upset . . . Then suddenly Colonel Henry Algernon, breathily moving toward Alfred, bringing the emotion of the situation to the breaking point, putting his hand on Alfred's shoulder and saying, "All right, I'm with you," then turning toward the family and saying, "I think I understand how Alfred feels when he says he wants to buy the company. I hereby give notice that I'm in favor of it and want you to give him a chance."

It was now up to Alfred to get going. He rushed out of the room where the family was assembled, jumped into his car and hurried to 2033 Delaware Avenue in Wilmington. There lived one of his cousins, Coleman du Pont. Evidently Alfred had kept Coleman in touch with the move the family was contemplating.* But now

* I learned from a good source that in the Coleman du Pont family they willingly related how, in this whole incident, Alfred merely played a role that Coleman had dreamed up for him. However, Pierre S., toward the end of his life, asked what there was to this story, replied: "Nothing could be further from the truth. It was Alfred, and Alfred alone, who took the initiative and intervened. Without him the

it appeared that Alfred's counterproposal, and above all Henry Algernon's support of it, had thrown them a little off balance. Having succeeded in calming Alfred, Coleman got on the phone and called Lorain, Ohio. He asked to speak to their cousin Pierre Samuel du Pont, for whom he had gotten the job of president of the Johnson Company, a steel business in the field of street railways. Pierre was told what had happened, and he agreed to take the first train to Wilmington.

The next day Alfred I., Coleman, and Pierre S., all first cousins, locked themselves up in the living room of Swamp Hall, Alfred's estate. Out of this long and mysterious conference evolved the agreement that was to be submitted to the family:

(1) Instead of a straight cash payment of 12 million dollars, shareholders would immediately receive (as token payment and in order to facilitate the legal formalities of transferring the securities) only $100 for each of the 21 shares in their collective possession, that is, $2100 all told. The balance of the 12 million dollars would be accounted for in a number of time payments plus 4 per cent interest, to be paid out of company earnings.

As guarantee, the old shareholders would be given stock in the new company, which they would have a right to keep if they preferred to stay with the business

Du Pont Co. would certainly have fallen into the hands of Laflin & Rand."

rather than be reimbursed in cash for their investment in the old firm.

(2) Once the old company was dissolved, it would be replaced immediately by a new company with Coleman as president. Alfred I. would be vice-president, Pierre S. would have the title of treasurer, and one seat, that of secretary, would be given to the ailing Charles I. in deference to the old Eugene faction.*

This Youth Plan was accepted without further discussion. Colonel Henry Algernon du Pont approved it; and as was traditional, the family followed the leader in matters where company interest was at stake.

A few days later, while making a tour of the company office, Pierre S. ran into Francis G., whom the family called "Uncle Frank." Uncle Frank had Pierre come into his office. The morning mail had just been laid out. Uncle Frank, pointing to it, said to Pierre: "It's all yours now." And with that he went out . . . but not without wishing his successor good luck. It was in this simple fashion, with no further formalities, that control of the company changed hands on February 23, 1902.

During the next two weeks, the three cousins went to work to try to find out just how much the business was actually worth. They themselves did not have the least idea, and the senior faction, who for the sake of

---

* Charles I. died before taking over this position and it was given to Alexis, II, son of the late president, Eugene.

form had assigned the E. I. Du Pont de Nemours Co., at the time of its incorporation, a capitalization of 12 million dollars, were equally in the dark. They came to the conclusion that the tangible property, money in the bank, recoverable contracts and the amount of orders on hand, plus stock in other powder plants held in company coffers, probably represented double the 12 million dollars that had to be paid out. This examination completed, Coleman went to the Seniors, and told them that: (1) the old company would be taken over for $15,-360,000, not for 12 million; (2) 12 million dollars in bonds bearing 4 per cent interest and $3,360,000 in new stock would be issued; (3) the 12 million dollars in bonds would be divided up pro rata among the old shareholders, besides the 33,600 shares of common stock with a par value of $100; and (4) 85,800 additional shares of preferred stock, to be progressively freed by the liquidation of the bonds, would belong to the newcomers. Of these, Coleman reserved 43,400 for himself, Pierre S. would have 21,200, Alfred 21,200 (plus his 3000 shares of common stock as an old shareholder).

Coleman had got the lion's share, and his partners made no attempt to have it any other way. Alfred realized that without Coleman, proven man of action, the Seniors would never have gone along with a plan so risky. In their eyes Coleman was the man to make it prosper. As for Pierre S., he had nothing to lose. He had neither Coleman's prestige nor Alfred's money; and this deal let him in on the ground floor and gave him the promise of a block of securities costing him absolutely nothing.

Pierre Samuel du Pont (II), sometimes called Pierre S., sometimes Pierre, of whom much will be said in ensuing chapters, was the oldest son of the Lammot who had been killed in the Repauno explosion. He and his first cousins Alfred I. and Coleman all were grandchildren of the cultivated, French-born Alfred Victor. In this fashion did the Alfred Victor branch — the senior branch of the family — get back what had been taken from them the day General Henry received the scepter of authority from the weak hands of his older brother, Alfred Victor. Now Alfred Victor's three grandchildren, the Triumvirate of brilliant cousins, were miraculously back on the scene. Each was completely different from the other two.

Alfred I., thirty-eight years old, was the only one of the trio who had made a career in the company in the du Pont tradition, that is, by working his way up the ladder, including a stint as a common laborer. As for Pierre S., he had left the Carney Point laboratories in 1899, in the conviction that there was no future for him in the Du Pont Company. He was as calm, close-mouthed and cautious as Alfred I. was impulsive and excitable.

Coleman — also thirty-eight — got his independent character from his father, Antoine Bidermann du Pont. It had been because he was unwilling to knuckle under to his Uncle Henry's dictatorial authority that Antoine Bidermann du Pont had left the company to try his luck in Kentucky. He had married Miss Ellen Coleman; hence the given name of his oldest son, who was better known by the nickname Coly. Though he had fallen far short of building up a business on the Du Pont Company scale, Coly had done very well for himself. A six-foot-four giant of a man, weighing 250 pounds, Coleman was more suited for boxing, wrestling, football and horseplay than for science and letters, but he had graduated from the Massachusetts Institute of Technology with a degree in mining engineering. Afterwards he had gone back to Kentucky, where his dynamism and practical business sense had accomplished wonders. Becoming superintendent of the Central Coal & Iron Company, he had teamed up with two other businessmen, Arthur Moxham and Tom Johnson, to regain control of the Johnson Company, where he had placed his cousin Pierre. Moxham, gray and self-effacing as a provincial bailiff, had a genius for making deals. Coly regarded him as his mentor.

As the treasurer of the Triumvirate, Pierre's greatest surprise when he took inventory of the old Eleuthère-Irénée du Pont Company was occasioned by the fact that Du Pont assets as such represented hardly more than 40 per cent of the total net worth. The remaining assets were in the form of blocs of shares scattered among innumerable companies making powder and explosives. Another singularity: Hazard Powder Company, 100 per cent controlled by Du Pont, was in much the same situation. At least 35 per cent of Hazard's capital was invested in theoretically competitive companies. Finally, Eugene and the General had so thoroughly intermingled Du Pont interests with those of Laflin & Rand that this latter firm held a minority interest in thirteen companies where Du Pont held the majority interest! Of the twenty-two explosives companies of any consequence existing in America, fifteen were more or less completely subsidiary to Du Pont and Laflin & Rand, and all owned blocks of stock in the seven supposed independents! This arrangement would be fine if Laflin & Rand indefinitely continued its fruitful association with Du Pont. But supposing the opposite happened? The Triumvirate, having turned this question over and over in their minds, decided that it would be the prudent thing to buy Laflin & Rand.

In October, 1902, Coleman offered Laflin & Rand 4 million dollars for the business. The offer was accepted. But an arrangement would be set up as in the case of the Du Pont Company — nothing or very little on immediate account, the remainder in bonds guaranteed by new stock. A financing company, the Delaware Securities Company, was set up by Pierre Samuel to float the bonds. No reason existed any longer for preserving a network of companies controlled from a distance. The Powder Trust had lost its usefulness since the passage of the Sherman Antitrust Act. By a stroke of the pen, the Gunpowder Trade Association was abolished. The companies controlled by Du Pont were dissolved and became a new corporation of E. I. Du Pont de Nemours Powder Company, again controlled by the parent firm.

The Wilmington Triumvirate believed in concentration of power, like so many other magnates whose methods were much the same as their own. John D. Rockefeller had "organized" the petroleum industry in this manner; Carnegie, steel; Philip Armour and Gustavus Swift, meat-packing; Guggenheim, copper; McCormick, farm machinery; Duke, tobacco; Vanderbilt, railroads. These maneuvers were effected with the assistance of financiers like Harriman, Hill, Gould, and above all Pierpont Morgan.

There was nothing original about the Du Pont combines except the truly astonishing manner in which Coleman handled money matters. He had something in common with the prestidigitator and card-trick artist, whose talents Coleman had cultivated as a hobby since youth. Add to this the gift of gab of a likable conjurer, and it will be understood how, by actually putting out only $2100, he had got away with the Du Pont business, worth at least 15 million dollars, and how, with only $2000 in working cash, he had taken over Laflin & Rand.*

Consciously or unconsciously, there was something of Barnum in Coleman. Everything had gone so smoothly that less than six months after seizing the Du Pont reins, the gigantic Coleman controlled 56 per cent of the United States explosives industry.

It is interesting to note that these grandstand plays were always followed by a methodical reorganization of the newly acquired company. At this point the two technicians, Pierre S. on finances and Alfred I. on questions of manufacture, came into their own. Both were solidly attached to family tradition and to their little native heath of Delaware, whereas Coly, born in Kentucky, cared not a straw about these ties and thoroughly disliked Wilmington.

This indifference came to light when Coleman, who was perishing of boredom in Wilmington, suggested that the old powder sheds of the Eleutherian Mills be shut down and that company headquarters be moved to New York. Pierre and Alfred, horrified, refused to go along with this sacrilegious proposition. Alfred took on the job of modernizing the plant on the banks of the

---

* The Delaware Securities Company had been incorporated with a fictitious capitalization of 4 million dollars. Equally imaginary was the capitalization of the Delaware Investment Trust incorporated at the same time for the purpose of buying the Moosic Powder Trust, a Laflin & Rand affiliate. President of these two financing companies was Arthur Moxham, Coly's partner in Kentucky.

Brandywine and the only change that Coly effected in the location of offices was to have them installed in the larger Equitable Trust Building in Wilmington, only ten minutes walking distance from the railroad station where trains left for New York and Washington. The shift was made in December, 1902.

The structure originally built by Eugene to accommodate the company offices exists to this day, and now serves as the home of Mrs. E. Paul du Pont. Two eprouvettes can be seen on either side of the porch, together with some of the balls used in these little howitzers at the end of the last century to bear witness by the distance of their flight to the excellence of Du Pont products.

The three cousins had a scientific cast of mind which made them aware that the manufacture of explosives was only an incidental aspect of industrial chemistry, a field which appeared to have unlimited possibilities. Two new research labs were created, as well as a new division, under "old man Moxham's" direction, to convert technologists' findings into actual production. It was Moxham who advised the Triumvirs to buy their first chemical company, International Smokeless Powder & Chemical, main products of which were lacquers and varnishes derived from nitrocellulose.

In 1903, recognizing that the system of individual management was not yielding enough return for an enterprise of such importance as his, Coleman proposed going over to a system of collective management. An executive committee was formed over which Coleman presided, assisted by Moxham, Pierre S., Alfred I., Haskell, Barksdale and Francis I. du Pont, a nephew of the late president, Eugene. All committee members were automatically members also of the company board of directors. The du Ponts still counted in point of numbers, but were no longer alone. Nevertheless, to be on the safe side, the family took precautions to prevent any sudden loss of leadership, such as had threatened on two occasions when the General and Eugene had almost been killed in accidents. Two of the younger du Ponts — A. Felix and Eugene, Jr. — were invested by Coleman with important responsibilities, and two of Pierre Samuel's brothers, Irénée and Lammot, came into the company.

In 1905, company operations, centralized thanks to measures instituted by the Triumvirate, were placed under the aegis of a new company, incorporated in Delaware like the one in 1902, but this time with a capital of 59.5 million dollars. It went without saying that the periodically maturing bonds were regularly paid off, likewise the 4 per cent dividend to holders of common stock and 5 per cent to holders of preferred stock. In 1907 Pierre announced to the Executive Committee that dividends paid on shares held in the company portfolio had risen to 10.3 million dollars. Thus comfortable reserves were at the firm's disposal. Only one member of the Senior faction still survived to admire the work of the new group: Colonel Henry Algernon. And he lived in Washington more than in Wilmington, since he was a senator from Delaware.

Behind this brilliant façade, however, troubles were brewing which the family itself could sense, but of which the general public was unaware. Alfred I., whose eccentricities had turned the company elders against him, was getting along badly with his wife. Several years earlier, when he took William's side upon the latter's excommunication by the family after his marital breakup, Alfred may have been thinking of a divorce for himself. At any rate, about 1903, while still married, he was taken by a passion for one of his young cousins, Alicia Bradford, a sportive girl with flashing green eyes and a heavy head of dark hair. The family gossips were somewhat subdued after her marriage to George Maddox, an employee of Du Pont. When Alfred I. was finally free to marry Alicia, people whispered he paid the husband one million dollars to quit town. On October 16, 1906, a Wilmington paper owned by Alfred published a sensational front-page story: "Alfred I. du Pont has just married in New York his cousin Alicia Maddox. The couple have just left on a trip in a 70 h.p. French car." With an ingenuousness we can only admire, Alfred had believed that the family would accept his divorce and remarriage as *faits accomplis*. His honeymoon trip over, he returned to his office in the Equitable Building in Wilmington as if nothing had happened. But the minute Coly was told Alfred had come back, he went looking for him and informed him that the "family would never stand for what he had done." He would have to resign. And it would be preferable for all concerned, moreover, if he moved out of town. Alfred was furious. He retorted that his personal affairs were his own business and no one else's and demanded that he be left strictly alone. If he was going to react this way, peace was out of the question. War within the family broke out and, as is usual with such struggles, it was to be implacable.

Alfred's first wrongdoing was to get divorced, his second to marry Alicia, whose conduct had given rise to vicious gossip. His third breach — this one unforgivable — was to have given his adventures vulgar publicity. Even Judge Bradford, Alicia's own father, himself married to a du Pont, anathematized his daughter. Leighton Coleman, an Episcopalian bishop married to another du Pont, did the same.

Alfred I. had always had an unbeatable reputation for originality. Had not his passion for music led him to form two bands in Wilmington, in which he played the cornet or clarinet in parades on national holidays? Mixing like this with his employees, was he not taking sides against his own class, who, traditionally, had always kept their distance from their workers, while at the same time treating them paternalistically?

Long hard of hearing, Alfred, forty years old in 1904, had become almost stone-deaf, and had through an accident lost the sight of one eye. After his marriage to Alicia in 1906 he obstinately kept coming to his office every day, where only the help spoke a word to him. In the evenings he went to inspect, with childish joy, the high wall enclosing the 300-acre property he had bought at Hedgeville, near Wilmington, the future site of his dream-castle, Nemours, which was to cost more than 2 million dollars. When they were installed at Nemours he was so furious because the ladies of Wilmington refused to come calling on Alicia that he then topped this wall with broken glass, to "keep them out."

The newspapers overflowed with accounts of Alfred's case. The Associated Press published every scrap of news about it, and a Philadelphia daily, the *North American*, put out a lurid story headed: "War of the Women Panics Delaware."

Psychoanalysts would probably explain Alfred's unstable and aggressive character by going back to his orphaned childhood and his fear, at the age of twelve, of being forced by the company to leave Swamp Hall, the parental home, to which he was fiercely attached. His Uncle Henry had wanted to separate the brothers and sisters and turn over Swamp Hall to a larger family. Alfred barricaded the doors and threatened violence if this was carried out. It was the defense of the young against the old — a defense of the small group against the family authority. It seems a logical conclusion that he confused in his mind the family authority, which he had fought against, with the many social taboos which he equally refused to follow. Later on, his brother Maurice, even more confused than he, was to commit suicide.

Alfred was a classic persecutor-persecuted type, handicapped by an isolating deafness. His instinct was not so much to destroy himself as to destroy everything, including his own household. He tried to deny the paternity of his own son and himself gave the orders to the wreckers to raze his adored Swamp Hall, which by now belonged to him. We do not propose to dwell at too great length on these incidents in the life of this grandson of Alfred Victor. However, it is impossible to ignore them, since they are part of the family history and inseparable, too, from the history of the company, which also had to endure the assaults of public curiosity.

The Sherman Act dated from 1890, but it was not until the turn of the century that it was to be frequently — and seriously — applied by President Theodore Roosevelt, who declared: "As far as the antitrust laws go, they will be enforced, and will not be compromised, except on the basis that the government wins. . . ."

In 1907, Roosevelt, through the Department of Justice, filed suit against the E. I. Du Pont Company on charges of having violated the Sherman Antitrust Act.

The government worked up a formidable case, basing its bill of particulars on information provided by a former employee of Hazard Powder by the name of R. Stuart Waddell, who had reason to complain of the du Ponts. Waddell claimed that they had sold the United States government powder at 75 cents a pound which had cost them only 31 cents to make. Hearing this, Congress and the press became aroused. Under these circumstances it would have been unwise to allow Alfred, now an enemy, to retain the post of command he held as chairman of Du Pont's finance committee. Using Alfred's deafness as a pretext, the executive committee discharged him and named Pierre S. in his place. Shortly afterwards, Coleman fell sick, and Pierre S. was made provisional president of the company. Alfred was still manager in charge of black powder production. But Pierre Samuel took this title away from him, too, and gave the job to his own brother Lammot. Now Alfred had only the title of a vice-president, with no authority, but he was still a large stockholder.

In 1911 the court handed down its decision. It found the Du Pont Company guilty as charged. Alfred was of the opinion that the matter should be let go at that.

But a majority of the executive committee felt the decision should be appealed.

Disheartened and out of a job, now that he had been stripped of his duties one by one, Alfred went with his wife in 1911 to live in Paris. He was a rich man, with an annual income of $400,000. Furthermore, he had foreseen correctly when he advised the company to accept the court's verdict. The du Ponts lost their appeal. They received an order to dissolve their organization as contrary to the Sherman Act.

Since their accession the Triumvirate had caused the Du Pont Company to absorb 64 explosives companies; they also controlled 69 others. It was difficult at this late date to revive companies that no longer existed, and difficult, too, to grant autonomy to the ones Coly had got under his thumb. A curious thing now occurred: The Army and Navy Departments issued a request that the Du Pont smokeless powder monopoly be permitted to continue. National defense would gain nothing, they said, quite the contrary, if the monopoly were taken away from the du Ponts. And it was a privilege they had never abused. There was agitation in Congress, but in the end the "elect of the people," content with having broken the Powder Trust, let the administration settle the question according to its lights. The solution finally adopted in 1911, and imposed on Du Pont, had three points:

(1) The E. I. Du Pont de Nemours Co. would keep

twelve black powder plants, five making dynamite and three making smokeless powder for the armed forces.

(2) It would divest itself completely of another group made up of eight black powder and three dynamite plants, which would retain the right to make use of hunting powder manufacturing patents held by Laflin & Rand. This latter grouping would take the name of Hercules Powder Company.

(3) A third group composed of six black powder and four dynamite plants would be organized under the name of Atlas Powder Company.*

Financial arrangements providing appropriate reimbursement for the Du Pont Company now followed. There was never any question of spoliation.

Even after all this, Du Pont de Nemours was still the largest explosives manufacturer in the United States. But in 1913, stockholders felt the blow to their interests dealt by the government: the $12 dividend of the preceding year dropped to $8.

As a matter of curiosity we pass along this information taken from the Annual Report for the year 1910 (signed T. C. du Pont): dividends which in 1904 had been ½ per cent had attained 3 per cent by 1905, 6½ per cent by 1906, 7¾ per cent by 1909 and 12 per cent by 1910!

---

* These three companies still exist today. Atlas Powder recently decided to take the name of Atlas Chemical Industries, Inc., as more suitably reflecting its actual production line.

8

On World War Scale

I find it less hazardous to write about the past than the present.

MONTAIGNE
Essais, I. 21

THOUGH NOW in mediocre health, Coleman du Pont was not a man to be satisfied with a domain cut down to size by government whim. Along with his Wilmington activities, he had been taking a burning interest in gigantic speculations with building companies. He had been one of the partners (with President Taft's brother) in the building syndicate which put up the Hotel MacAlpin in New York. This hotel had the double advantage of being near the Pennsylvania Station, where Wilmington trains came in, and close to Broadway, with its theaters and nightclubs and its actors and actresses, in whose company Coleman loved to spend his evenings. His apartment on the twenty-first floor of the hotel became famous for his fabulous parties. Coleman, like Henry, was called General — Coleman was commander of the Delaware Militia.

In 1912 Coleman had the Du Pont Company buy two blocks in the heart of Wilmington to put up a fourteen-story Du Pont Building. One part would be used as a theater, another part as a hotel, and the rest as office space. For the provincials of Wilmington and their almost as provincial Philadelphia neighbors, this was a monumental move, but it hardly satisfied the New Yorker that Coleman du Pont had now become. ("You never catch big fish except in deep water," he used to say.)

In 1913 he threw himself into a project that was more in his style: the construction, right on Broadway, of a forty-story skyscraper, the Equitable Building, where 15,000 people would be employed in 2300 offices. The first Equitable building was erected in 1867 by Henry Hyde at 120 Broadway, "on the southeast corner of Broadway and Cedar Street, opposite Trinity Churchyard." It was seven stories high and Equitable was, according to the *History of Architecture and the Building Trades of Greater New York,* "the first corporation bold enough to undertake a great office building in connection with its own place of business." In 1899, when Hyde died, the four sides of the Equitable Building were draped from roof to floor with black crepe! The heir of Henry Hyde, James Hazen Hyde, sold his controlling interest in Equitable to another flamboyant gentleman, Thomas Fortune Ryan, king of tobacco. In 1909, Ryan sold Equitable to J. Pierpont Morgan. On January 9, 1912, a fire destroyed the Equitable Building. It was such a catastrophe that the next morning six leading New York banks closed their doors and the Stock Exchange suspended the deliveries of securities. Only a businessman like Coleman had the same stature as the big ones who made Equitable famous. He bought for $13,500,000 the plot and the ruins of 120 Broadway and built what was to be the biggest skyscraper in the world. In April, 1914, this grandiose construction (40 stories high, 40 acres of floor space to be rented, 63 Otis elevators, 33,000 tons of steel) was begun.

Sickness was lying in wait for Coleman. He had been stricken, he knew, by cancer, and would have to undergo another operation. At the beginning of 1914, once again back on his feet, he returned to Wilmington, having held on to his title of president of E. I. Du Pont de Nemours & Co. He was at his desk in June, when Archduke Francis-Ferdinand was assassinated, and a month later, when World War I broke out. Self-styled experts in Washington unhesitatingly predicted that the war would be short, since the combatants had such powerful means of destruction at their command. This was the opinion, too, of American industrialists. It is likely that people holding responsible positions at Du Pont thought the same.

If the company worked a little harder than usual

from July to September it was because the United States War Department, as a precautionary measure, began to stockpile powder. It was not until October of the same year that an emissary of the Russian government appeared at the Wilmington offices and, having been introduced to Pierre du Pont, explained the reason for his visit: St. Petersburg wanted to know how long it would take and how much it would cost for Du Pont to deliver 480 tons of trinitrotoluene (TNT). Some days later a French official came to place an order for 4000 tons of propellant powder and 600 of guncotton. The tempo of Allied orders increased from one week to the next. By January 1 the company had on its books orders for 8000 tons of gunpowder, 1500 of guncotton and 1300 of TNT.

By now everyone realized that the war would last, bogged down as it was in thousands of miles of trenches on both Eastern and Western fronts. The Allied powers also estimated that the productive capacity of their own explosives plants would be inadequate.

Coleman had gone back into the hospital at the end of August, and Pierre had once more taken over the reins. His responsibilities were to become all the more onerous, since the war among nations had not put an end to the du Pont family war, which had now taken an extraordinary turn.

In December, 1914, Coleman had written from the hospital to his cousin Pierre that he would like to sell

20,000 Du Pont shares to certain of his employees at a favorable price. By so doing he hoped both to recompense and to attach more closely to Du Pont interests the employees from whom an exceptional effort would be expected.

Ever since 1904 the Du Pont Company, on Coleman's initiative, had had in effect a bonus system whereby high-echelon company men were allowed to become stockholders. In 1907, the company books showed that as a result, 217 of the 899 total stockholders were family members and 682 were employees and outsiders. In 1910 the number of stockholders had risen to 1695, of whom 764 were Du Pont de Nemours personnel. This trend was to continue.

Coleman was offering 20,000 shares at a market price of $160. Alfred, still a member of the board, was informed by Pierre of what was in prospect. Alfred expostulated that it should not be necessary for the outsiders to pay more than $125 per share. Pierre S. called a meeting of the finance committee on December 23 to see what should be done. The only ones to show up for the meeting were Alfred and his cousin William, and since the latter automatically sided with Alfred, the result was a foregone conclusion. Pierre, a minority of one, deemed Coleman's offer rejected.

Recently one of the du Ponts supposedly familiar with events of the past said this: "Why did Coleman offer these 20,000 shares? And above all why did he offer them at a time when, with Allied orders flowing in, he could anticipate great profits as their value rose? My uncle knew better than anyone else what he was doing. Like so many sportsmen, he loved fair play. To him it seemed unjust to hold on to so many securities, when he'd given less and less of his time to the company for the past three years. He wanted to do his fellow workers a good turn." Others who also knew Coly well told me this explanation was probably correct, but it must be added that at this time Coleman needed cash for his personal speculations.

It may seem tedious to place so much stress on the details of the internal affairs of the Du Pont Company in this winter of 1914-1915, when so many men were dying in war. But these matters take on more importance in light of the fact that Germany, too, after its abortive offensives in France and Russia, found itself short of gunpowder, and, having got wind of quarrels within the family, secretly instructed the German ambassador in Washington to try, through go-betweens, to seize control of Du Pont.

In certain circles close to Wall Street a rumor spread that no less a brokerage firm than Kuhn, Loeb was trying, on the German government's behalf, to buy up all the Du Pont shares it could find in the market. Also, a certain Captain von Rintelen had contacted Amory Haskell in Wilmington to find out whether there was any way of buying a large block of stock directly.

London and Paris were naturally aware of this development. In December there was genuine alarm among the Allies when it was learned that Coleman's 20,000 shares might be going up for sale. An agent of the British government, Mr. Kraftmeyer, officially in the employ of Nobel, Ltd., took passage on the *Lusitania*. To receive him at company headquarters in Wilmington an emergency council was convoked, composed of Pierre and Irénée du Pont, flanked by Colonel Edmund G. Buckner, at that time Du Pont's liaison man with the War Department. It has never transpired, so far as I know, what went on in the meeting. Nevertheless, it is known that Mr. Kraftmeyer was a much calmer man when he left than when he arrived. If anyone is astonished that the question of Du Pont loyalty should even be brought up at all, it must not be forgotten that during this period the United States was neutral and American industrialists had the right to sell to whom they pleased. At all events, it appears now that Pierre's intention was to buy back himself all of his cousin's shares, and that Germany, in consequence, had scarcely any chance of grabbing a majority.

Coly had written in exasperation to Alfred: "Be so kind as to let me know how many of your own shares you are willing to let go at the market price of $125 that you claim is fair. As soon as I have your answer, I will give up the same number as you at this price." Alfred did not reply. Du Pont shares were not even quoted on the New York Stock Exchange in 1914, but in January, 1915, they were being traded over the counter in Wall Street at $200. Coleman meanwhile had withdrawn his first proposition. In February he informed Pierre that he was prepared to give up 30,000 or even 40,000 of his shares at the $200 market price, on condition that the company resell them to the employees. His secretary, who delivered the new offer, added: "The General warns that if you continue to hold off, the price will rise to $300."

On February 28, 1915, under the headline: "The General Sells His Interest in the Du Pont Co.," Alfred read in a Wilmington newspaper (a rival of his own) an article announcing "the purchase by Pierre du Pont and various persons in the Company" of all of Coleman's shares. He and his cousins William and Philip, who were in his camp, reacted with amazement and anger when they heard the news. All three asked for an explanation. Pierre undertook to oblige. From him they learned that the purchase had been carried out, as the newspaper had said, in the name of a syndicate composed of several members of the company, not in the name of the Du Pont Company itself. Members of the syndicate were Pierre and his two brothers Irénée and Lammot, Pierre's brother-in-law Robert Carpenter, his cousins Alexis, III, and Felix du Pont, and finally Pierre's business confidant and intimate associate John Jacob Raskob. The syndicate now owned 63,214 shares of common stock costing $200 a share and 13,989 shares of preferred stock acquired at a price of $85. Even without counting the shares already owned by the three brothers, the two cousins, and Carpenter, there were more than enough to ensure the syndicate a majority in the company. Cost of the operation, which had been directed by Pierre, had been exactly $13,831,865, of which 8 million dollars had been paid in cash to Coleman. The remainder was to be paid in a series of notes spread over seven years and carrying 6 per cent interest. "Other than this," Pierre specified, "we had to pay out $500,000 in commissions to intermediaries."

Among these "intermediaries," it need hardly be said, was the banker Pierpont Morgan, with whom Raskob, acting for the syndicate, had floated a loan of 8.5 million dollars. "Morgan would not have lent you so much money on a personal basis," Alfred said to Pierre. "It had to be in your capacity as director of the Du Pont Company. Therefore, it is the company which actually owns Coleman's block of shares. I insist you return them to the company." Pierre refused to admit this interpretation. The company board of directors met to judge the dispute and said Pierre was right. They voted that he take the president's chair vacated by Coleman. Once he had this vote of confidence, Pierre had them adopt his plan for reorganizing the business.

A holding company, the Du Pont Securities Co., was created. This company, capitalized at 240 million dollars, would control E. I. Du Pont de Nemours & Co. Another company, the Christiana Securities Corporation, which had been organized by Pierre's genius, would be put in charge of financing the purchase of Coleman's securities, it being understood that syndicate members would deposit in the corporation the majority of shares taken in their name by Du Pont Securities. Key executives in the Du Pont de Nemours division were now offered — to keep them happy — a certain number of shares of Du Pont Securities, on condition that they agree to remain at least one more year in company service.

In March, 1915, the market price of the new Du Pont de Nemours shares (two for one of the old) was $293. Before the end of the year the price had risen to $450; thus former stockholders' shares were now worth $900 as against $200 before. Even the malcontents eliminated by the deal, including Alfred, should have recognized the advantage of this. But no; one of them, Philip du Pont, nephew of the late president Eugene, brought court action in their behalf against the syndicate. In 1916 Alfred lost his vice-president's title and his seat on the board. Even his office was taken away from him.

Thus in definitive and brutal fashion ended the Du Pont Company career of this singular personage without whom, in 1902, the family would have lost the business. To get revenge, in 1916, with his cousin William, Alfred bought the Delaware Trust Company, a bank he intended to make into a competitor of the Wilmington Trust Company, the Du Pont bank.

Principal clients of Delaware Trust, naturally, were Alfred and members of the family who had taken his side. The considerable amount of capital of this little group was to be augmented by the deposits of a large number of company employees, among whom "Mr. Alfred" had always been very popular. This much, at any rate, was a source of annoyance to the rest of the du Ponts. As a further vexation, Alfred built the new Delaware Trust building several stories higher than the Du Pont Company building nearby. Some years ago in Hong Kong I saw a similar incident in the Orient. The Red Chinese government bank won "la guerre de l'altitude" against the Bank of England. In Wilmington the rebel fortress similarly dominated the battlefield. And people devoured Alfred's *Morning News,* to get contradictory advices on the war of the du Ponts.

When Colonel Henry Algernon du Pont was running for re-election to the Senate, an attempt was made to promote Alfred's candidacy against him. Actually Alfred himself did not enter the lists, but he did have his newspapers support the Colonel's opponent and his press campaign did a good deal to ensure the Colonel's defeat. Alfred seemed to attract complication and paradox. Before the war his oldest daughter had married a German, who naturally was fighting in the ranks of the Imperial army. And in 1916, he adopted a little French girl, Denise, whose father had been killed at Verdun.

Not until 1919 did the action of du Pont *vs.* du Pont reach its epilogue with a Supreme Court decision that dismissed the case of Philip and his partisans. Thus two wars ended the same year, one in Wilmington and one at Versailles. But it was to take a long time for the enemy du Pont clans to forget the horrors of their war. In 1921 the governor of Delaware appointed Coleman to the Senate seat vacated by Senator Wolcott. When his term ended in 1923 he ran for re-election. Against him, Alfred supported a well-known Democrat, Thomas F. Bayard (married to Elizabeth du Pont, Philip's sister), and Bayard was elected. The great Coly had to wait for another vacancy and times of peace to obtain the seat he coveted.

Alfred apparently sensed the crash coming in 1929, and at great profit he sold 2 million dollars' worth of securities and wisely salted away the proceeds. Thus he became one of those rare American businessmen who liquidated their stock holdings before the debacle. He profited by making exceedingly advantageous loans and by acquisitions at distress prices. He built a magnificent estate, Epping Forest, near Jacksonville, Florida, and divided his time between there and Nemours, the fairy castle of the beloved Alicia, who had died in 1918 when Alfred was fifty-four years old. Meanwhile Alfred again got married, this time to a Southern schoolteacher, Jessie Ball, distantly related to George Washington. This lady, whom the family called "Cousin Jessie," knew how to keep her husband happy. Intelligent and gracious, it was she who did the most to effect a reconciliation with his relatives and to make both sides forget the past.

Alfred died an enormously rich man in 1935, having gained, after he was dropped by Du Pont, almost as much money in Florida speculations as from the ancestral company.

"Cousin Jessie" turned out to be a super-business-woman. She took over Alfred's old office in the Delaware Trust building and from there managed her financial deals together with her brother, Edward Ball. These operations were backed by a group of Florida banks which Alfred had picked up for a ridiculously low price in the 1930's. The holding company, known as the Florida National Bank Group, mainly controlled paper and lumber companies. Recently Edward Ball and "Cousin Jessie" succeeded in getting control of a railroad company — the Florida East Coast Railway — which had been experiencing serious difficulties; and they are now in the process of reorganizing it. The capital of Alfred's trust, which they administer, has grown considerably, and now appears to be more than 400 million dollars. This trust will be for the use of the Foundation for Crippled Children after their death. Like her late husband, Mrs. Alfred du Pont divides her time between Wilmington — she lives at the great house of Nemours — and Florida.

With the money left by Alfred to this foundation an ultramodern, very spacious children's hospital has been built in a section of the park at Nemours, and later the great mansion itself and indeed the whole estate will serve to expand this model hospital. Mainly for the poor, the hospital is so marvelous that the rich are envious, for not even a du Pont can enter ahead of the poorest child. Near the hospital a high carillon tower, dedicated by Alfred to his parents, contains his tomb. Interred with him is his mongrel dog Yip, which died some days after him.

From the beginning of January, 1915, the Du Pont Company management began to realize that their explosives plants, however big they might be, were no longer big enough to meet Allied needs. Either the company would have to expand, or orders would have to be refused. Colonel Buckner was commissioned to speak plainly to Allied representatives. Since 1904 he had held important posts with Du Pont and was now in charge of powder sales. "This war," he told them, "is not of our making. If there are risks to be taken, then it's up to you to take them."* The past had not been forgotten at the Du Pont Company. They knew by experience that "once out of danger, the saint gets the brushoff," that governments which in time of war order explosives from

* Cf. William Dutton, *Du Pont: One Hundred and Forty Years,* p. 225.

specialized industries let these same industries upon the advent of peace make shift as best they can in recovering capital invested in expanded production facilities. Colonel Buckner handed the Allies an agreement which offered the following terms: (1) They must pay 50 per cent down on the order; and (2) the prices would be such that no matter what happened the company would be able swiftly to recoup money laid out on new plants.

Thus covered, the Du Pont management plunged without hesitation into a preplanned expansion program. In October, 1914, the maximum capacity of the Du Pont plants did not exceed 330 tons of TNT a month. By the end of February, 1915, they were turning out 1200 tons. Each ensuing year, production facilities for all kinds of powder (in 1915 there were 90 different kinds of explosives) were to be perfected in a spectacular fashion. Thanks to its laboratory research, Du Pont had introduced a process for drying the powder which speeded up their delivery rate by two months. In December, 1916, Du Pont plants were producing explosives at a rate of 100,000 tons a month, compared to 4200 tons two years before.

When the United States declared war in June, 1917, the government had made no provision for dealing with this new situation. President Wilson, almost up to the last moment, had virtually prohibited all preparation for war. In 1915, let us not forget, this militantly "neutralist" President had reacted with fury when he learned that a group of officers at Fort Leavenworth had been advised to undertake a military planning study just in case the United States should become directly involved in the conflict. These officers worked with French Ecole Militaire maps of the Franco-Prussian War of 1870, since the American military authorities had none of their own of more recent date.

On April 20, 1917, the head of general military procurement called to Washington the presidents of the four largest explosives companies in the United States. He advised them that the government anticipated need for 3200 tons a month of explosives to meet the needs of the expeditionary force and the Navy. It was agreed — since it was imperative not to curtail Allied supplies — that three large plants would be built at government expense, one near Charleston, another near Nashville and a third near Louisville.

Pierre S., president of his company and now forty-seven years old, had, as noted earlier, organized the company into specialized departments. Fletcher Brown managed the smokeless powder division, Harry Haskell high explosives, Colonel Buckner contracts, and Major William G. Ramsay, up to his death in 1916, plant construction. Dr. Charles Reese directed research.

The question of price was a delicate matter. When the War Department had insisted on making Du Pont its sole supplier of smokeless powder, Congress had specified that the government was not to pay more than

53 cents a pound. The Allies, having had no alternative, had agreed on a price of $1 a pound. After the American government had settled on a price of 47½ cents, the Allies also profited from this price reduction. Fair enough, since capital invested by Du Pont had long since been reimbursed and since war costs were now being shared by all, including the United States.

Russia laid down her arms in October, 1917; hence several German armies were free to reinforce Germany's Western front after the Russian Revolution. General Pershing reported to President Wilson that the strength of the American Expeditionary Force should be swiftly expanded to a million men. In consequence, the April 20 estimates of explosives requirements had to be revised. A revision was further necessary because, according to a memorandum addressed to Washington by an American mission: "Working at full capacity, French plants are unable to deliver the 8500 tons of explosives indispensable for the French Army."

According to Colonel Buckner, the American government again summoned the principal explosives manufacturers to Washington and informed them that 115 million pounds of powder would be needed. "How much of this amount," it was asked, "can Du Pont furnish?" "All of it," Colonel Buckner replied. "And at a certain price, win or lose, of 47 cents a pound for all categories except small arms powder, and that at a price of 62 cents a pound." This was consistently the price charged the government by the Du Pont Company, according to Buckner, but agreements made with Du Pont competitors not so well equipped for mass production were higher.

Late in the autumn of 1917, the American mission headed by Colonel Edward M. House visited Europe especially to get for America a place on the Supreme War Council in the Interallied Conference. Colonel House was to tell the Allies — who were skeptical — that America was in the war as a full partner and to determine the most effective method in which she should cooperate. Two features colored the negotiations of Colonel House in London and in Paris: the growing need for American troops and the seriousness of the shipping situation. It was obvious that the German U-boats were so effective as to make American cooperation exceedingly difficult. The outlook for the transportation of both troops and munitions was extremely dark. At this point, the Allies assured Colonel House that the production of artillery itself (field, medium and heavy guns) was such in Europe in 1917 that France and Great Britain would be able to equip all the American divisions arriving in Europe during 1918. The French and British ammunition supply and reserves were enough to provide for the requirements of these divisions at least to June, 1918. The French and the British governments wanted only American help for supplies of propellants and high explosives. For this reason, it was necessary that American efforts concentrate on production of these supplies on the largest possible scale. An agreement was signed on these terms. At the outbreak of the war in 1914, the American producing capacity for smokeless powder was approximately 1,500,000 pounds a month. By the time the United States went to war, this capacity had been increased from 25 to 30 times, thanks to the Allied orders to U.S. manufacturers and especially to the Du Pont Powder Company. From the end of 1917 to November, 1918, America's production of propellants — the powder loaded in small cartridges or packed into the guns behind the projectiles — was practically equal to that of Great Britain and France together.

War production questions had become so complicated that a War Industries Board was formed in Washington to deal with them exclusively. Technologists in this new bureau said that the production goal should be a rate of 45,000 tons a month of explosives of all types in the United States, for both America and the Allies. But the production tonnages of all existing installations added up to only 26,000 tons. More plants, therefore, would be needed. Who would pay for them? The government would. But who would be in charge of construction — companies specializing in explosives manufacture, or contractor bureaus set up by the government? For a number of reasons Washington hesitated. Meanwhile the Du Pont Company got a War Department order to submit plans for a plant capable of producing 500 tons a day. The plans were drawn up, but were not finally accepted until four months later, since certain Congressmen suspected that the company was asking too high a price. In fact, it was not until the financier Bernard Baruch took over the direction of the War Industries Board that, after this dangerous loss of time, difficulties were finally ironed out and construction of the Old Hickory plant in Tennessee began.

The doors of the first of the Old Hickory installations opened in July, 1918, a month earlier than anticipated; eight others were successively finished ahead of the timetable. This powder plant, built on World War scale, cost the government 85 million dollars. Statisticians have estimated that 200,000 workers had to be mobilized to put up its 1112 production buildings, and in addition 3867 houses built to accommodate 30,000 people. This city of a plant, with churches, hospitals and schools, sprang from the ground between March and November, 1918. In addition to all this, nearly nine miles of railroad, as well as highways, streets and roads, had been built, not to mention a bridge about 490 feet long over the Cumberland River.

This spectacular industrial complex for the manufacture of explosives represented only part of the accomplishments of the Du Pont Engineering Company, which was commissioned to carry out a whole program of war plant construction for the government. Further, the government let out large contracts to E. I. Du Pont de

Nemours or its specialized affiliates not only for powders and explosives, but for shells, fuses, gas mask parts, and other such equipment.

Old Hickory was the most important plant built by Uncle Sam in World War I for increasing the munitions production in the United States. The second in importance was Nitro, near Charleston, West Virginia. It had a capacity of 625,000 pounds of smokeless powder a day and was operated by Hercules Powder. It is not surprising to see this company, which before 1912 was included in the Du Pont empire, occupying the second rank in the smokeless powder business. Another company which had been a part of Du Pont — Atlas Powder Co. — also became important in helping America fight the war. Three plants only in the United States were fabricating all the mercury fulminate for detonators, caps and primers. One belonged to Du Pont, one to Atlas Powder and the third to Aetna Powder Co. As in a classical play, all the actors were reunited on stage for the last act.

The November 11 armistice robbed Old Hickory of its *raison d'être* and resulted in the cancellation of 260 million dollars in contracts for Du Pont. If the war had gone on, the Du Pont Company would have been able to supply the Allies with as much as 300,000 tons of powder a year. From December, 1914, to November, 1918, four out of every ten shells fired by Allied artillery came from Du Pont.

9

From Delaware to Michigan

> There are three things to be
> considered about an organiza-
> tion: what it offers to the
> public, what it offers to its
> own rank and file, and what
> it offers to its leaders.
>
> BERTRAND RUSSELL
> *Understanding History*

IN DU PONT's 1918 stockholders' report is this statement: "The Company now returns to its commercial
business consisting of lines of manufacture of previous
years." For a long time, Pierre S., now forty-eight, had
been reflecting on what would happen when the war
was over. It was because of the war that his firm had
been catapulted up among the highest-ranking corporations in the world, and that it employed up to 100,000
workers, as many as a whole army of combatants. However, these were years when he wished he might direct
the business away from munitions, where it had made
a fortune, toward other activities. In the first place, he

was pacific at heart, and it was painful to him to be called a "merchant of death." In the second place, he was discerning enough to recognize that from year to year the use of explosives would be increasingly limited, now that the day of the pioneer and clearer of land was past. Ever since 1914 there had been articles making unpleasant reference to Du Pont activities. One which appeared in *Harper's Weekly* had gone so far as to declare that "the du Ponts have stolen the secrets of smokeless powder manufacture from the American government and have sold them to the Germans" — in effect accusing them of treason.

And whenever the du Ponts went to court to clear their name, no matter what they did, they ended up by feeding the very rumors that were such a sore point with the family. After the war these rumors were to increase even more, nourished by the difficulties that Du Pont had run into in Congress and on the War Industries Board, by their acuteness in buying up the Old Hickory plant from the government at such a low price, and above all, by stories about their fantastic war profits.

It would be tedious to develop at length the arguments pro and con of accusers and accused. But it is a fact that after the war the government took possession of the Old Hickory plant which Du Pont had run for it and all the land belonging to Old Hickory. The Nashville Industrial Corporation then bought the property from the government, and proceeded to resell the major portion of the land and buildings to E. I. du Pont de Nemours & Co. for $800,000. Testimony given before a Congressional investigating committee revealed that all the government got back from the liquidation of Old Hickory installations and material costing 85 million dollars was 3.5 million dollars.

Lammot du Pont undertook to defend these war profits with a candid and exhaustive examination of the subject in a report called *The Du Pont Co. and Munitions,* which appeared in 1934. His main points were as follows:

(1) It is reasonable to hope that some day mankind will do away with war, but for the time being the fact must be faced that "wars are an undeniable fact of human existence" and that nations must arm.

(2) A century of experience has taught us that profit is the determining incentive in industrial enterprises filling human wants.

(3) The manufacture of military explosives, unfortunately a necessity, is subject to the same general economic laws as any other industrial operation.

(4) E. I. du Pont de Nemours & Co. supplied governments with explosives.

(5) These governments found this arrangement to their advantage, since Du Pont products were such that "not one powder delivery during the whole war

was of poor quality." This was not the case with other companies.

(6) Allied orders before the entry of the United States into the war were regarded as of a usual business character. Prices exacted were in line with the belief that the war would be short and that money invested in expansion would have to be written off in a few months. But when it was seen the war would not be short, the price, originally set at $1 a pound, dropped to 97 cents in 1916, to 55 cents later that year, and still further, to 53 cents, after 1917.

(7) From 1914 to 1919 the company made a profit in round figures of about 59 million dollars a year, as compared with a little more than an average 5 million dollars a year before the war.

It is interesting to compare this with another text on the same subject.* Its author, Colonel Buckner, could certainly speak with authority, since it was he who had been charged with drawing up munitions contracts on the company's behalf. "When this awful war first started in Europe and we were asked to quote terms on which we could help in furnishing powder . . . it was a mixed question what the company could safely undertake. . . . The cost of labor and the attitude of labor toward supplying munitions to the Allies was unsettled. We had in this country a large element strongly in sym-

* Address by Colonel Buckner at the General Sales Convention in Atlantic City, June 19, 1918. Brochure in the New York Public Library.

pathy with Germany, which created a great hazard."

Explaining that, at the time, Du Pont production capacity was only 12 million pounds of powder a year and that the orders called for an annual production of 440 million pounds, Colonel Buckner went on to say:

"The demand was especially for small granulations and small arms powder, including '3 Field Gun Powder,' for which our prewar price had been 80 cents a pound." According to him, the excuse for raising the price to $1 was that this 20 per cent increase was to take care of increased risk, and had been a reasonable move on the company's part.

Buckner continued: "It was a foreign war. . . . At the time we were quoting prices and terms to the Allies, President Wilson was contending that it was not our fight, that we had nothing at stake; neither had anything been done against our interest or our honor and that we should remain neutral. It was only natural this company should take its cue from the note preached by President Wilson which was so popular throughout the whole country as to have elected him to a second term. . . ." In summary Buckner opined that those who condemned Du Pont were unjust "because they are judging us by today's standard, which is righteously opposed to profiteering and excessive money-making out of war, and not by the standard which ruled at that time and which ruled the majority of the country. . . ."

As to the requirement that the Allies pay 50 per cent down and the rest on delivery — this was a hard bargain, but according to this energetic representative of Du Pont, in the long run everybody gained by it, since "it put the Du Pont Co. in a position both as to funds and confidence which eliminated all fears of loss or doubt as to the successful completion of the contracts by both parties to such degree that all limits were off and we were ready to accept any proposition involving any amount which contained these terms. . . ."

Colonel Buckner further said that Allied orders were so large that the Du Pont Company was able "to put a new plant in operation nearly every day" to meet its commitments! And were the Allies satisfied with their contracts with Du Pont? No doubt about it. J. P. Morgan had informed the Colonel that Lancy Nichols, just back from London, had said that Lord Moulton, head of the British Munitions Board, declared to him before witnesses that it was "because of the work done by J. P. Morgan in buying munitions, by Du Pont in manufacturing explosives and by Bethlehem Steel in supplying field-guns and howitzers that the Franco-British armies had been able to hold against the Germans in 1915." Colonel Buckner could adduce additional evidence. On one occasion he ran into the English General Hedlam at the home of Colonel McRoberts of the U. S. Ordnance Department. The General had said: "Let me assure you that the Du Pont Company has saved the

British Empire!" In his June, 1918, speech, Colonel Buckner added, to show that his company had been ready to make certain accommodations, "In 1915, because of difficulties England was having in getting dollars, we accepted for one year British government bonds amounting to $46,700,000 in payment of orders. And under the same conditions and for the same reason, we accepted $9,200,000 worth of French government bonds. And this was not all. When England and France first appealed to the U.S. to give them financial aid, asking for a loan of $500 million, Du Pont subscribed to Anglo-French bonds in the amount of $36,500,000. . . ."

In this same address, with a frankness comparable to Lammot du Pont's, Colonel Buckner made the following statement:

"I am proud to admit that we have made millions of dollars. If we had lost millions, our critics today who condemn us would laugh and call us idiots and fools and the Kaiser would have the laugh on this government because it was not prepared with powder. . . ."

The Colonel's summarizing figures give an idea of the magnitude of Du Pont's wartime activities:

"The total value of all contracts for military business to date [June, 1918] is $1,011,000,000. This represents 26 years of normal prewar business of the company. Compared with normal military commands in prewar business, this represents 276 years."

To all this it might be added that whereas World

War I did permit the Du Pont Company to make a lot of money and expand greatly, many other American corporations did the same. All America became an Allied arsenal at this time, and the result was to accelerate American industrialization to an undreamed-of degree. The acceleration was even more spectacular in World War II, and this prosperity, because of the need for reconstruction, continued long after the war.

What precisely do we mean by war profits? Only profits made by companies producing war materials during a war? Or do we include, too, profits made before or after these conflicts? Do these gains include stockholders' dividends, not forgetting speculative profits made on the stock exchanges, or the double salaries received by those in speed-up work? Nor is it true that direct profit in money is necessarily the only gain to be counted. Consider how many now famous public figures in the world owe their good fortune to war!

Pierre S. du Pont of course did not leave idle in the vault these millions of dollars of profits. First to benefit were the stockholders — a majority of them members of the family. Next, Pierre had the company buy lacquer and varnish plants, which gave them a place in the chemicals field. Finally, on the advice of his collaborator John Jakob Raskob, Pierre invested a considerable amount of Du Pont money in General Motors. Du Pont had thus made overtures in two fields of great promise for the future — as a direct result of the war.

Moreover — a measure of Pierre's astonishing business acumen — he even made money from the government's war surpluses: enormous stockpiles of powder and dynamite for which it had no further use. Pierre bought them back at a very low price and resold them to a number of state governments, including those of Georgia, Texas, Louisiana, and Florida, which needed them for various land-clearing and sanitation projects.

Mention of John Jakob Raskob is overdue, since it is impossible to discuss the affairs of Du Pont and General Motors without finding his fingers — like a modern Talleyrand's — in every pie.

Raskob's grandfather, Jakob, immigrating from Grossliechin, Germany, landed in America in 1845 and began a little cigar business in Buffalo. His father, John, continued in this field in Lockport, N.Y., where he married an Irish girl, Anna Frances Moran, and where John Jakob was born in 1879. It seems likely that John Jakob, one of four children, did not get far in school; according to his privately printed biography, the *Raskob-Green Record Book*, his education "was received in Lockport." It is certain, however, that sometime before 1900, Raskob was a streetcar conductor, and that he was in Lorain, Ohio, at the time Pierre Samuel du Pont was president of Johnson Company, which controlled the streetcar business. Could that be how Pierre S. had occasion to meet Raskob? I have been told by an old friend of these men that Pierre in fact urged Raskob to learn stenography, with the intention of giving him an office job. Raskob very soon became the president's personal secretary at Johnson. (A short five years later, when Raskob had his own office, he hired only men to assist him. One of his three personal secretaries, just before the 1929 crash, was the Texan Robert R. Young, who had been with General Motors since 1922. When Young persisted in advising "the Boss," as everybody called him, to sell out, Raskob got so angry he fired him!)

In 1902, when Pierre S. du Pont became a member of the Du Pont Triumvirate, he wrote to Raskob, who had also quit Johnson and was then in New York, offering him in Wilmington the same job he had had in Lorain. Always practical, Raskob wrote back: "I'll think about it. Send me a two-way ticket so I can come down and look things over." The return ticket was never used, and from personal secretary Raskob graduated to Pierre's adviser and confidant. In 1906, he married Helena Springer Green, a devout Roman Catholic like himself.

In 1909, Raskob bought from Alfred I. 1000 shares of Du Pont stock on the installment plan which was guaranteed by Pierre S. By 1911, he was the treasurer of the E. I. Du Pont de Nemours Company and the Raskob family was living in a grandiose château, Archmere, built by John Jakob on the outskirts of Wilmington. In 1915, Raskob received from Pierre S. 1250 more shares for his work on the deal involving the stock bought from Coleman.

Raskob in 1921 had thirteen children and many millions of dollars. His energy was boundless. Restless at Archmere, he decided on a place in Maryland. When he took his wife to admire the new house, she exclaimed: "Why, this is mostly halls!" So he named the place Mostly Halls. In 1931, Raskob was the head of a group, which included his friend Al Smith, who financed, at a cost of $40,948,000, the construction of the Empire State Building.

As the children grew up, Mrs. Raskob patiently covered fifteen dining room chairs in needlepoint with the name of each child, her own, and John Jakob's, to denote which chair belonged to whom. Years later, this unique collection was given to Cardinal Spellman, and it is said to be in daily use by him. Other legacies also went to the Roman Catholic Church, among them Mostly Halls and Archmere. Today, every morning a fresh bouquet of red roses is placed under the portrait of Cardinal Spellman in the Raskob Pavilion of St. Vincent's Hospital in New York — an offering in memory of Raskob from his daughter Josephine.

In the Du Pont Company's 1918 annual report, Pierre praised sixteen of his colleagues who, in his opinion, had contributed most to Du Pont's expansion. Nine of

these people were members of the executive committee. Many had worked so hard during the war years
that they were now worn out. Certain others were un-
suited for doing their best anywhere but in explosives
manufacture. Pierre proposed that most of the present
members of the executive committee transfer to the
financial committee and that the executive committee
be reorganized with new blood. As for himself, he
would relinquish the responsibilities of the company
presidency, turning the position over to his brother
Irénée, and limit himself to supervising company activities from the higher and less absorbing post of chairman of the board. In April, 1919, his other brother, Lammot, was made chairman of the executive committee,
into which was now inducted Walter S. Carpenter, then
only thirty-one years old.

Today it seems obvious that it was a good idea to
invest in General Motors. But in 1914, when Pierre S.
personally bought — upon the recommendation of John
J. Raskob — 2000 shares of General Motors, this move
entailed daring risks. In 1899, at least 80 automobile
companies were officially registered in the United
States, though the majority of them employed only a
handful of workers, men who had formerly been in
carriage works. It was in 1900 that the first auto accident was recorded in New York — a woman killed while
crossing Broadway.

Although from 1902 to 1912 more than 2000 different

makes of cars were produced, at the start of the First World War only a few companies survived. Standing out among the survivors were two: one started by Henry Ford, the other by William Crapo Durant. In 1908 Ford had come out with the popular Model T, selling for less than $1000. This was indeed revolutionary, when we note that Woodrow Wilson, then president of Princeton University, had written: "The motor car presents a picture of the arrogance of wealth, with all its independence and carelessness." Before Woodrow Wilson became President of the United States, Ford had made this "picture of arrogance" a commonplace means of helping workers and farmers earn a living.

William Crapo Durant, Ford's rival and no less imaginative than he, was of French descent,* like the du Ponts. In 1898 while still very young, Durant bought for $50 a shop where horse-drawn carriages were made by hand. He organized it on a mass-production basis so as to produce nearly 50,000 carriages a year, and by 1904 he was rich. Casting about, he found in Flint, Michigan, a mechanic who was making three cars a year in a shed. The man lacked the money to go on with his work, and Durant bought his trademark: Buick Motors Corporation. His idea was to use the assembly line techniques of carriage manufacture in making auto

* Durant's grandfather, a seaman, had settled in Massachusetts as a boat-builder. His father made a fortune in Michigan lumber mills.

bodies. Starting with a capital of only $75,000, he put out a call for funds which in less than a week — for Durant inspired confidence — was answered by a subscription of 1.5 million dollars. With this backing, it was an easy matter for him to launch his Buick. Thanks to this venture, the little town of Flint by 1908 was making 8000 cars a year and had become an important American industrial center.

That same year, 1908, Durant incorporated in New Jersey a holding company capitalized at 12 million dollars, which he christened General Motors. This was around the period when Coleman du Pont was building up his domain by mergers, and by the same means Durant got hold of a number of other makes, such as Cadillac, Oldsmobile, Oakland and Weston, which he placed, like Buick, under General Motors control. He came close, too, to adding the Ford make to his collection when he offered its discouraged founder 8 million dollars to sell out. Durant's ambition was to make 500,-000 cars a year. Pierpont Morgan was skeptical and refused to lend him the money he needed to merge Ford and General Motors resources. Durant next tried Lee Higginson with no success and was turned down as flatly by J. and W. Seligman.

Durant's bankers, shortsighted people, had considered the 8-million-dollar price tag too high. It must be said in their defense, however, that the audacity of their client's mergers was staggering. Durant juggled millions as others gambled with pennies. In 1910, for example, it took a group of Boston bankers a long time to make up their minds to lend him the 14 million dollars he urgently needed, and in order to guarantee the loan they took over such a large block of General Motors shares that they became majority stockholders. As a consequence, Durant was supplanted as president of General Motors by Charles Nash.

Four years later Durant financed the French manufacturer Louis Chevrolet (who used to race in his own cars) and soon bought him out. Then Durant founded the Chevrolet Motor Company, incorporated in Wilmington, but took care to keep this new make entirely for himself and out of General Motors. At this same time he was buying back in the market, in the name of Chevrolet Motor Company, 450,000 shares of General Motors. By 1916, the Boston bankers and Durant were about equal partners in General Motors.

It may have been on a trip to Wilmington for Chevrolet purposes that Durant met in 1915 Hamilton Barksdale, son-in-law of a du Pont and the man the Du Pont Company had turned to under stress in 1902 when they were in need of someone to supervise their contemplated liquidation. Barksdale, Raskob, Pierre du Pont, Durant. . . . This connection, in any case, was made. Durant named Barksdale president of the Chevrolet Motor Corporation and sold the Du Pont Company 3000 shares of General Motors. Pierre du Pont, John

Raskob, J. A. Haskell and Lammot Belin du Pont were made directors of General Motors, with Pierre S. as chairman of the board. It was a clever way, Durant thought, of interposing a "third force" to balance the situation between himself and his bankers. It is said in Wilmington that members of the Du Pont Company were so little convinced of the wisdom of picking up the General Motors shares that wise Pierre's proposal was twice rejected. It was Raskob who insisted in 1917 that Pierre make a third and last try to get the proposition to a vote. It was on this last attempt that the proposal was accepted by the board.

On December 21, 1917, the executive and finance committees of Du Pont approved the acquisition of common stock in General Motors and Chevrolet Motors Company (which controlled General Motors) in the amount of 25 million dollars. By March, 1918, General Industries, Inc., whose stock was held by Du Pont, had purchased approximately 23 per cent of the common stock of these companies. Between 1918 and 1920, through General Industries, "Wilmington people" (as Durant called the Du Pont de Nemours Company and the du Pont family) owned almost 24 per cent of the outstanding stock of General Motors. In 1920, Pierre S. and Durant dissolved the old General Motors Corporation of New Jersey and replaced it with a new corporation, with the same name, registered in Delaware with a capitalization of $120,600,000. One wonders what would have been the future of General Motors if the president of Du Pont at this time had been Coleman the Grandiose instead of Pierre the Wise. Managed by those masters of manipulation, Coleman and Durant, General Motors' scope might have made today's giant seem puny — or it might have gone the way of the Marmon.

People who knew both Durant and Pierre S. predicted that their partnership would not last long. It was a miracle that Raskob was able to hold the association in balance for two years. In 1917, thanks to government orders, General Motors business had been particularly profitable (350 million dollars net). In 1918, however, the incorrigible Durant was again short of money. He proposed to Du Pont that if they would lend him 25 million dollars they could share with him the management of General Motors. Naturally Pierre S. accepted the offer. Some months later, Durant asked for another 25 million. They granted him the loan, but put a complete Du Pont team in positions of command at General Motors — indeed, they took over the entire executive and financial committees. Except for his own stock, all that Durant retained was the one position just suited to his genius, director of General Motors production and promotion, working within the framework of a budget determined by Pierre S., who had now become the real head of the business.

It was at this point that General Motors absorbed Chevrolet; thus it became the largest automobile company in the world, with a capital of more than a billion dollars.

The postwar depression proved fatal for William C. Durant. A gambler, he had taken long shots in Wall Street, and found himself owing 27 million dollars. Once more he turned to his partner, Pierre S. du Pont, who for 35 million dollars picked up the 33 per cent interest that the unhappy Durant still retained in the company. In 1920, Pierre S. was elected president of General Motors, replacing Durant, who disappeared from the picture completely.

Thus, after 1920 the du Ponts simultaneously controlled the principal Detroit automobile company and the most powerful explosives company in America. They also had a solid position in the chemicals industry. And it is even said that Pierre had invested 14 million dollars in the United States Steel Company at the suggestion of Pierpont Morgan. Their empire was immense, but fragile, too, since the American economy as a whole had developed too rapidly during the war years and lacked a firm base.

The Du Pont Company's good fortune was to have had, when he was needed, the right man for the job, Pierre Samuel du Pont, a superior organizer and skillful financier, who made it his first concern to get General Motors solidly on its feet. He reorganized the corporation from top to bottom, decentralized its departments and cut out useless expenditures. He even reduced the

executive committee to four members — himself, Raskob, Haskell and Alfred Sloan.

At this point, an additional and more romantic du
Pont contribution to automotive history should be
noted. If it is true that Pierre S. had the good judgment
to invest in General Motors a part of the enormous war
profits of E. I. Du Pont de Nemours & Co., it is no less
true that there was another du Pont, his cousin E. Paul,
who also understood the brilliant future of the automobile.

In 1914 E. Paul had joined the Biddle Motor Car
Company of Philadelphia; but the war interrupted this
venture, and in 1917 he went into the explosives business and also became president of the Delaware Marine
Motor Company, where he was perfectly at home because of his pronounced mechanical talents. After the
war, he and a former collaborator in the Biddle Motor
Car Company, Arthur M. Maris, decided to return to
their first love, the automobile. Thus, partly in the house
of E. Paul du Pont, partly in a local workshop on Commerce Street in Wilmington, they assembled their first
model — a de luxe automobile called the Du Pont. This
car was shown in 1919 at the Automobile Show in New
York and was a sensation. It is hardly possible that this
publicity pleased Pierre Samuel and his team, who were
launching the cars of General Motors and not "that
one" coming from the house of Cousin Paul. It is said

that Pierre Samuel quietly persuaded the Delaware Motor Car Company to build its beautiful car outside of Delaware. It is true that the workshop was moved sixteen miles away, to Moore, Pennsylvania. The production setup of this company was, to say the least, complicated. The office continued to be in Wilmington, closed bodies came from Philadelphia, open bodies came from Springfield, Massachusetts, some parts were coming from Detroit, and the final assembly, paint and trim was done in Moore. Even with this peculiar system, Du Pont was delivering about 150 cars a month, priced at $4000, by the fall of 1920. Was it only the name of Du Pont which attracted such celebrities as Will Rogers, Jack Dempsey, Eugene O'Neill? In the opinion of W. Bowman, "The famous name of Du Pont added prestige to an automobile that did not deserve it." On the other hand, a well-known amateur racer of this era, Charles Moran (today a partner of Francis I. du Pont & Co.), obviously had another opinion since he raced a Du Pont at Le Mans and at Indianapolis against the best in the world. Neither was it the opinion of Stanley Yost, the expert on the subject of ancient cars to whom I am indebted for a great part of my information. According to him, "It was not just another car — it was an engineering masterpiece."

Financially speaking, E. Paul's venture ran into trouble in 1929 and disappeared in 1933. A visitor to Mrs. E. Paul du Pont today can see, on entering her house, just off the entrance, the machine shop where her husband worked on his first car. It is still set up as he left it.

Until 1940 Pierre remained president of Du Pont, but he had resigned in 1923 as president of General Motors — perhaps not entirely of his own volition, but to protect himself from accusations that the power of the du Ponts, broken once by the government in 1912, had been restored and was again contravening the law.

Since 1920 a Department of Justice investigating commission had been examining everything in Du Pont files pertaining to war orders. Not until 1925 did the Attorney General conclude that nothing of a reprehensible nature had been disclosed. But in 1927 the Department of Justice, flanked by the Federal Trade Commission, again took up the cudgel. This time, objection centered about relations between Du Pont and General Motors. The closed inquiry ended in absolution for the company. In 1934, under the administration of Franklin D. Roosevelt, there was a new investigation, this time an open one by a Senate investigating committee on the "activities of the munitions merchants" in general and of Du Pont in particular. This was inconclusive, and all that remains is an interminable record printed at the American taxpayers' expense. One remarkable fact is that the Senate committee's chief investigator was Alger Hiss. From 1941 to 1944 other

even more politically oriented Congressional committees — the La Follette and the Nye-Vandenberg, on
which Vandenberg opposed the majority — scrutinized
Du Pont activities as munitions-makers, as supporters
of fascist and anti-Semitic groups, as belonging to international cartels (Imperial Chemical and I. G. Farben),
and so on.

The du Ponts, it is true, were not the only ones who
came under fire from Congress. In 1942 had not another committee headed by Democratic Senator Harry
S. Truman called the Standard Oil Company of New
Jersey traitors?* According to him, this company had
refused to make use of its patents for the manufacture
of artificial rubber in order to protect the German firms
from whom they had bought them.

More incredibly, during the munitions investigation
of the seventy-third Congress an investigator on a committee of inquiry was claiming to have proof that the
Du Pont Company had helped Germany secretly rearm
— and this with the complicity of Secretary of Commerce Herbert Hoover! Another Senate committee investigating lobbies, headed by Hugo Black, asserted
that the Liberty League and its affiliates, among them
the militantly anti-Semitic Sentinels of the Republic,
were largely financed by individual du Ponts. Finally,
Democratic Representative John M. Coffee inserted in

* Truman Committee's war investigation (1942). The newspaper
P.M. headlined the news "Standard Oil Accused of Treason."

the *Congressional Record* a statement in which he came to the conclusion that Du Pont, General Motors and other American corporations "have conspired with Baron von Tippleskirch in an attempt to sign a pact of alliance between Hitlerist Germany and leading Republican businessmen in the United States." The alleged history of the relationship between the house of Du Pont and the Hitlerist movement figures in a curious document entitled *Monograph I, Economic and Political Aspects of International Cartels, Committee on Military Affairs, 1944.* How much truth is there to these allegations? The elected representatives of the people of the United States have the advantage over newspapermen of being able to say what they want without having to prove their accusations in court.

On June 30, 1949, the antitrust division of the Department of Justice filed suit against Du Pont. The case went to trial in Chicago in 1952, and in 1954 District Judge Walter J. La Buy dismissed the government complaint. Acting on behalf of the government was an army of attorneys helping Stanley N. Barnes, Assistant Attorney General. On the side of Du Pont were the representatives of Covington & Burling of Washington, D.C., and those of Sidley, Austin, Burgess & Smith, from Chicago. At least forty-five lawyers were assembled to defend the U.S. Rubber Co., General Motors, Wilmington Trust Co., Delaware Realty Corp. and Christiana Securities. The government appealed to the Supreme

Court. In 1957, the Court ruled that although officers of Du Pont and General Motors had acted without intention to violate the Sherman and Clayton Acts, Du Pont's ownership of 23 per cent of G.M. stock "created a reasonable probability" that this relationship could lead to a monopoly. Later on, the Supreme Court ruled that Du Pont must divest itself of its G.M. shares within ten years.

Under the heading "Moscow vs. Du Pont," the *Wall Street Journal* noted in September, 1961, that *Izvestia*, an official Soviet government publication, called Du Pont "the cannon king of the U.S. . . . whose wish is the Law in Washington." And Du Pont snapped: "In and around the Supreme Court it would have them rolling in the aisles."

Some idea can be gained of the value of these early Du Pont investments in General Motors by considering the fact that the original shares were exchanged for new ones in 1924 on a four-for-one basis. This operation gave them 1,330,800 shares, which became 9,981,000 shares through a free distribution of stock in 1935. Further splits effected between 1935 and 1955 again doubled this number. A final readjustment, in 1956, brought total Du Pont holdings to 63 million shares! At the Wall Street market price at the time Judge La Buy found for Du Pont against the government, the value of this investment was $1,055,000,000. But the Supreme Court did not share the judge's opinion. Its decision was that Du Pont would have to divest itself of its General Motors stock. But how? Sixty-three million shares of the largest corporation in the world cannot just be dumped on the market — even over a period of ten years — without injuring the stockholders and risking a collapse in Wall Street.

To avoid this catastrophe, they thought of distributing all shares among the stockholders in the Du Pont Company. This turned out to be impractical, because from the interpretation of the Supreme Court, the Treasury Department would be the principal beneficiary, taking a billion dollars in capital gains taxes.

Democratic Senator Frear of Delaware, in sympathy with their plight, introduced a bill in 1959, applicable to this case only, to amend the Internal Revenue Code. It was on its way to passage when Frear failed to be re-elected. A new version of the derailed Frear bill was passed by the Senate in January, 1962, leaving the next move to Judge La Buy.

The court action brought against Du Pont because of its tie-in with General Motors was equally aimed at the allegedly excessive Du Pont holdings in U.S. Rubber. Between 1913 and 1927 Irénée and Lammot du Pont bought large blocks of shares in this corporation at a speculative market price on their personal account. With relatives and friends they formed a syndicate, the Rubber Securities Company Trust, which made a bid to get a controlling interest in U.S. Rubber Company.

Lammot du Pont Copeland, said to be principal stockholder
in the Du Pont Company, in 1960

Dr. Charles M. A. Stine, Director of Research during
the period of the invention of Duco, neoprene, and nylon

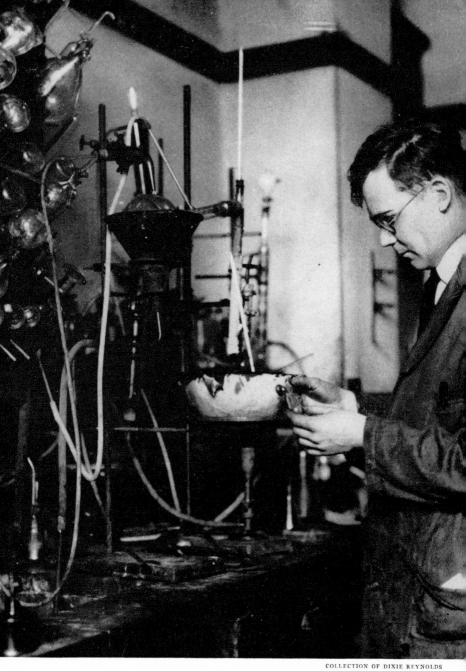

Wallace Carothers, inventor of nylon in 1935

Eleuthère Irénée du Pont, at right, with his son, and his father,
the son of Coleman du Pont, in 1952

Irénée du Pont, Jr., and his son in 1954

The brothers A. Rhett and Edmond du Pont in their Wall Street office

CERTIFICAT.

Compagnie *d'Amérique.*

ACTION DE DEUX MILLE DOLLARS OU PIASTRES FORTES.

N.° 304.

est intéressé pour la présente Action,

N.°   dans la Société en commandite, formée sous la raison de Du Pont (de Nemours) père et fils, et compagnie, pour l'acquisition, l'amélioration et la revente des terres, le commerce rural, et la commission du commerce maritime dans les États-Unis de l'Amérique: aux clauses, conditions, avantages, dividendes et partage de bénéfices mentionnés en l'ACTE DE SOCIÉTÉ, signé le vingt-huit floréal de l'an six de la République Française.

La présente Action est aliénable, successible et transmissible par voie de Transfert sur les registres de la Société.

Délivrée à   le

Pour la Compagnie

Administrateurs,   Syndics.

A $2000 Du Pont Père et Fils Company stock certificate
nobody wanted to buy in 1799

Henry Belin du Pont, with his wife Emily, in 1960

Pierre S. du Pont (II) in his patio at Longwood Gardens, in 1959

9026

CHRISTIANA SECURITIES COMPANY

DELAWARE REALTY & INVESTMENT COMPANY

One door, two employees, a billion dollars:
the Christiana Securities Company

A public showplace: the gigantic hothouses at Longwood Gardens

Bois des Fossés (U.S.A.), home of Pierre S. du Pont, III

Granogue, home of Irénée du Pont, dean of the family in 1962

Saint Amour, home of Lammot du Pont, brother of Pierre S. (II) and Irénée

The chateau of Philip du Pont, who sued the Pierre S. group in 1915

In the family cemetery, the graves of Messire Pierre-Samuel du Pont
and his grandson, Admiral Samuel Francis du Pont

Main square in Wilmington, with Caesar Rodney on his horse,
the hotel Du Pont in the background and piped music at noontime

Nicole du Pont, 1959 debutante

According to Judge La Buy, "Irénée du Pont invited Cyrus Eaton, a banker, to join in the purchase of Rubber Securities stock and sell his U.S. Rubber shares to Rubber Securities. It appears from the record that Eaton, through Continental Shares, had about 100,000 shares of the United States Rubber stock. Irénée du Pont testified that he thought it would be a very good thing to have him 'definitely working with us rather than against us.' Eaton refused the invitation."

The case against Du Pont, as it pertained to U.S. Rubber, was dismissed.

10

"Better Things for Better Living . . ."

Eleuthère-Irénée du Pont, who founded the Du Pont Company in 1802, was a chemist; and nearly all the members of the family who later played a role in the business were trained for chemistry. But Pierre S. changed the company's basic character when he made certain investments for security's sake from the profits of his explosives manufactures.

As early as 1915 Pierre had set up a special Development Department, headed by R. R. Carpenter, which was charged with studying the records of chemical products firms which would eventually be for sale. On the recommendation of this department Pierre Samuel had the company buy up several lacquer and varnish firms. During the early years of the war the Development Department's attention had been drawn to the difficulties the American chemical industry was experiencing because of its heavy dependence on foreign imports, particularly from Germany. What would happen if America were drawn into the fight against Germany? In 1914 three quarters of all coal-tar dyes used not only in the United States but throughout the world came from dye plants beyond the Rhine. American imports were soon cut off by the blockade. This caused such difficulty that in 1915 Washington got permission from London to have some Dutch cargo vessels, loaded at Hamburg, pass through the mine fields and the Allied blockade so that the United States government might have enough German dye to print its paper currency and stamps.

Some time before this the German submarine *Deutschland,* basically for German publicity purposes, had slipped through the blockade to deliver a token cargo of pharmaceutical products and dyes to the United States.

The American paper, textile and paint industries as a whole suffered heavily from the dye shortage, and the manufacture of drugs created serious problems. For Du Pont, 1916 was a memorable year, since it was at this time that their technologists, working in what was a rather modest research center, began to look for a solution to the problem of making dyestuffs. By February, 1917, they had made such progress that the executive committee allocated an initial $600,000 to the organic chemistry division of the Chemical Department to build a plant for the manufacture of synthetic indigo. Shortly afterwards, Pierre's brother Lammot left the management of the black powder department to take over the organic chemistry operation.

The manufacture of dyes was centralized at Deepwater Point, across the Delaware River from Wilmington. An outlay of 7 million dollars had been anticipated for this enterprise, but by 1925, some 43 million dollars had been spent. For some years this business had to be run at a loss, at first because the market was not yet organized, and later because of costly errors arising from American chemists' lack of experience.

In 1918 all German manufacturing patents registered in Washington were sequestered under the so-called Trading with the Enemy Act. In 1919 those relating to chemistry were assigned to the Chemical Foundation, and this organization was charged with distributing them among interested American companies. Needless to say, Du Pont claimed its share. And it is probably true that it was in great measure thanks to these patents that from 1923 on the company was finally able to produce dyes of a quality comparable to those made in Germany by I. G. Farben Industries. Ever since, Du Pont has continued to be the most important source of supply in this field for American industry and, through its affiliates, for foreign industry as well. And undoubtedly it was through its interest in the manufacture of dyestuffs that the company was led to get a foothold — and a solid one — in still another field — plastics.

Among the members of the Du Pont executive committee, as reorganized by Pierre S. after World War I, was Donaldson Brown. This gentleman had connections with two brothers of Strasbourg origin who lived in New York, Albert and Henri Blum, who had established a silk dye business called the Alexander Dye Works, Inc., and were well acquainted with the Gillets of Lyons, France, as well as with the management of the Comptoir Général des Textiles Artificiels.

In 1913, the Comptoir des Textiles Artificiels in Paris had founded the Société Anonyme de la Cellophane to exploit the patents for an extraordinary product invented in 1906 by the Swiss engineer Jacques Brandenberger,* who had worked for several years in France. This material, which had been given the poetic name of Cellophane, was expensive, and had consequently achieved scant popularity in France. During the First World War, however, it had been used in fairly large amounts in the manufacture of gas masks.

In 1920 Henri Blum brought back a sample of the material for Donaldson Brown. Brown, immediately fascinated by it, persuaded Blum to go back immediately to France to negotiate the purchase of the Cellophane patent from the Gillets for the United States. Du Pont then formed the Du Pont Cellophane Co., in which Henri Blum was rewarded with a directorship. A son of Henri Blum, who recounted this story, also re-

* The first experimentation toward cellophane was that of two Englishmen, Cross and Bevan, in 1894.

calls: "I remember this Du Pont company most vividly, because when I was a youngster Dad always gave me the ten-dollar gold piece he received at each board meeting; and I still have them." Brandenberger came to Buffalo in 1924 to inaugurate the first cellophane plant manufacturing his discovery on a commercial scale. Cellophane caught on rather quickly — first, in 1925, among Philadelphia confectioners for their luxury products, then among bakeries, and in rapid succession, all over America, the chewing gum, cigarette and food industries. Transparency, purity, hygiene . . . Cellophane has become to Europeans a sort of symbol of the American way of life. Du Pont manufactures moisture-proof cellophane in five plants strategically located near the principal areas of American consumption. Their total production capacity is around 285 million pounds a year. (The total of Du Pont's competitors — Olin Mathieson and American Viscose — is about 260 million pounds.) Cellophane is still the leader over all other competitive types of packaging film.

It was through its contacts with dye manufacturers that Du Pont got the idea of making cellophane. But cellophane is closely related chemically to viscose, and therefore to cellulose — and the company had long been interested in cellulose since Du Pont made guncotton from this substance. The company found innumerable applications for nitrates of cellulose in lacquers and varnishes, impregnation of tissues, photographic film, plastic materials, synthetic filaments, and so on. In 1910 Du Pont had bought the Fabrikoid Company, owner of a patent for covering cotton with a lacquer film based on nitrocellulose so as to obtain a kind of artificial leather. In 1925 Du Pont bought the Viscaloid Company to make a synthetic product related to celluloid (invented in 1901) under the name of Pyralin.

Du Pont's entry into the plastics field was followed by giant steps in the field of organic chemistry, where the basic element is carbon, and in inorganic chemistry as well (sulphuric acid, ammonia, caustic soda, chlorine, and so forth). Among the principal firms bought by Du Pont were the National Ammonia Company (1925) and, above all, Grasselli Chemicals, founded by an Italian chemist, Eugene Grasselli, who had built a plant for the manufacture of sulphuric acid in Ohio in 1839. His company had grown greatly in scope, and had as one of its big customers the oil refineries of John D. Rockefeller, when Lammot du Pont bought the Grasselli Company in 1928 for 60 million dollars. Until recent years it constituted a separate Du Pont division, but it has now been completely absorbed. Today Du Pont is among the largest producers of high- and low-density polyethylene, acrylic and polyvinyl butyral resins. It is indeed the leader in production of high-performance plastics.

The science of chemistry, with its innumerable innovations, has given us the means to simplify and beautify our existence. The poetic words it has adopted to label its creations sound like something from the pen of Maeterlinck — Ethylene, Isoprene, Butadiene, Fluor, Lucite, Penicillin, Phenidrone, Hydralizine, Ethanole . . .

Chemical products derived from natural gas and petroleum, which in 1924 amounted to only 75 tons a year in the United States, in 1959 amounted to 2500 products totaling 22 million tons. The vice-president and general manager of the Standard Oil Company of New Jersey has stated that, out of the 3 billion dollars invested in 1960 by the United States chemical industry, 1850 million dollars were in petro-chemical installations. According to him, 50 per cent of all Du Pont business is based on petroleum or natural gas. In 1958 the American chemical industry manufactured 1275 million dollars' worth of resin plastics, 1629 million of paints, lacquers and varnishes, 235 million of detergents, 1501 million of chemicals for agricultural use, 1327 million of synthetic fibers and 544 million of synthetic rubber. The Du Pont public relations department at Wilmington claims that the company makes at least 1200 different products. Du Pont is still a big producer of titanium dioxide and titanium pigments used in paints. It is also one of eight American companies engaged in developing uses for columbium, another metal. As early as 1955 the Du Pont department specializing in metallic pigments had succeeded in the experimental

[218]

production of pure columbium. A plant near Baltimore will use processes developed in the laboratory for the production of columbium, or niobium (of which 90 per cent is used as an alloy in stainless steel and some of the carbon steels). Whether one is at home or in one's car, whether playing golf or tennis, fishing, playing football or baseball, opening a package of cigarettes, or bringing food home from the store in a protective wrapping, one inevitably uses Du Pont products. Women's slips, men's suits, eyeglasses — they are found in all of these. Yet most people are not conscious of this fact, since Du Pont, author of innumerable successes, disdains putting its signature on these products. It leaves to others the business of making use of them.

These prodigious results in the domain of technological discovery are the fruit of costly effort. Mr. Crawford H. Greenewalt, president of Du Pont, wrote recently: "The proportion of dollars spent in research as compared with investment in plant construction is on the order of one to three. This proportion has become almost constant in recent years. For our part, during the last 25 years we have spent $600 million in our laboratories, not counting the cost of installations. We have spent $1,800 million for new plant and equipment. . . ." However, success is more than a question of more or less dollars expended. Chance or luck still plays its part.

Very likely neither Firestone nor Du Pont would have spent what they did on developing synthetic rubber had war not cut off their imports of natural rubber from the Far East. In 1925 Du Pont technicians, bypassing the German synthesis from acetone, got the idea from their experiments at Jackson's Laboratory of mixing diacetylene with latex to obtain a kind of rubber — a product which, however, had no practical use. They had arrived at this point when Dr. Elmer K. Bolton, director of the chemical section of the Du Pont Dye Department, happened to attend an American Chemical Society meeting. Also attending the same meeting was the Abbé Julius A. Nieuwland, professor of organic chemistry at the University of Notre Dame. This Belgian-born cleric, who had become an American citizen, had devised an ingenious system for opening his laboratory door by means of a foot pedal, since it was his habit to go about with arms loaded with books or flasks — and this same Abbé probably knew more than any other man in the United States about the mysteries of acetylene. Dr. Bolton, who had rounded out his studies at the Kaiser Wilhelm Institute in Berlin in 1915, had turned his attention to finding a way of making synthetic rubber after seeing the Germans, squeezed by the blockade, attempt to find a substitute for natural rubber.

The Abbé read a paper before his colleagues, including Dr. Bolton, telling about an experiment he had performed with acetylene, using copper as a catalyst.

At once he had obtained an oily yellow substance which he called di-vinylacetylene. Moreover — and this was the point which particularly impressed Dr. Bolton — during the reaction the Abbé had detected, by its odor, the presence of a known gas, monovinyl acetylene. Dr. Bolton and Abbé Nieuwland put their heads together to try to make sense out of this phenomenon. The result was that the Notre Dame cleric, who himself had no commercial interest in the problem, agreed to have a Du Pont team of chemists collaborate in his work, including Wallace Carothers, F. B. Downing and Ira Williams. Out of this collaboration in 1929 came a practical method for the production of the gas monovinyl acetylene. From then on, only a few trials were needed to obtain a liquid named chloroprene, which had a structure analogous to that of the already known isoprene. The two substances were differentiated by the fact that chloroprene polymerized very much faster into an elastic state, and for certain uses it was much superior to natural rubber. The Du Pont Company announced the discovery of synthetic rubber at the time they were building a plant at Deepwater Point to manufacture it on commercial scale under the trade name of Neoprene. By 1939 an appreciable tonnage of neoprene was being used by industry. In 1941, after Pearl Harbor, the government requisitioned the plant and also financed the construction of a second one in Kentucky. The Abbé Nieuwland, I have been told, got his share of royalties for the invention of neoprene and donated them to the Congregation of the Holy Cross.

Chance figured even more notably in the discovery of Duco. In 1902 the Du Pont laboratories had reached a point where they were able to make cellulose lacquers on a limited scale. In 1920, after buying into General Motors, the Du Pont management naturally was thrown into contact with technical problems in the automobile field. One of these problems was to paint auto bodies in varying colors on the assembly lines, another to get away from the time-consuming process of painting the bodies by hand and then letting them slowly dry. In Wilmington, the possibility was considered of using cellulose lacquers, but the ones under manufacture were not applicable to auto use. One day at the Parlin Research Center in New Jersey, chemists were making a test on movie film. They had made the necessary preparation when an electric power failure interrupted their work. By chance they threw their preparation into a barrel of nitrocellulose outside the laboratory door, and forgot it. Three days later, one of them, Edmond M. Flaherty, remembered and went to retrieve the test material from the barrel. To his amazement, he discovered a syrupy liquid at the bottom of the container instead of the normally gelatinous nitrocellulose. Upon examination, this liquid proved to be exactly what they had been seeking for so long as a base for paint. The tech-

nicians noted that the barrel had remained three days
out in the courtyard in the glare of the sun. It was easy
to reproduce artificially the same conditions provided
by nature. Thus Duco was born, a true child of the sun.

There would be no end to it if one undertook to discuss all the things Du Pont makes. But one all-important
development must be included — the history of nylon,
a material appreciated by a Frenchman like myself as
being directly involved in our revival after the miseries
of German occupation. At last the atrocious cotton
or wool which for four years had disgraced the love-
liest legs disappeared. Equally remembered and appreciated by us Frenchmen is the awed astonishment at
the silence of the American army marching through
France. What contrast their synthetic rubber soles made
with the thunderous German boots! And what jealousy
we had of the nylon stockings carried in their gear, in-
struments of amorous conquest!

When Lammot du Pont became president of the com-
pany, succeeding his brother Irénée, Dr. Charles M. A.
Stine had earned the reputation in scientific circles of
being both a learned man and a bold spirit. Son of a
New England Lutheran minister, Dr. Stine joined Du
Pont in 1907 and became director of chemical products.
Lammot was not particularly surprised when, in 1927,
Dr. Stine made an astonishing proposal. In a large

American university there was a young genius of a chemist. Dr. Stine proposed that this man be asked to resign his academic position and take over the directorship of Du Pont's research laboratories, with the understanding that he could carry out his work regardless of the practical value it might or might not have for Du Pont. Carte blanche and very liberal treatment indeed, but Lammot agreed. This was how it came about that at the beginning of 1928 Dr. Stine led into the imposing office of the president and general manager of the Du Pont Company a diffident, myopic person — Dr. Wallace Carothers — come to take over his position as head of research.

Carothers was then thirty-one years old. Son of a Midwestern schoolteacher, he had at a very early age become passionately interested in chemistry. An exceptionally gifted youth, at nineteen he had written a monograph published by the *Journal of the American Chemical Society* on the work of Irving Langmuir and its application in the field of organic chemistry. As a result of this remarkable publication he received in 1920 a scholarship at the University of Illinois. Afterwards one of his professors took him as his assistant to the University of South Dakota, and while there he was offered and accepted a position at Harvard. Experts said his courses were excellent, but sometimes too learned for the students. A difficult personality, thin-skinned, impatient, nervous, he was less a professor than a scientific seeker with original views. At Du Pont, Carothers became head of a team of chemists who found him to be, if not an even-tempered superior, at any rate one whose scientific knowledge gained their admiration. It can be said that it was thanks to this team in general and to Carothers in particular that research undertaken at Dr. Bolton's instigation ended in the discovery of neoprene. But it seems it is uniquely to Carothers that we are indebted for the discovery of nylon.

While still at Harvard, Carothers had foreseen what might be expected from the polymerization of substances of high molecular weight. In April, 1930, one of his fellow-workers at Wilmington found in his test tube a product of singular elasticity instead of the crystalline sort of substance heretofore derived from chain polymerizations. From this event Carothers drew the conclusion that it was possible to synthesize "giant polymers" of the same type as leather, linen or silk. He called the new substance a superpolymer. The originality of Carothers's idea, according to the experts, lay in the fact that he used what are called difunctional organic acids to obtain the classic acid or base reactions in order to create synthetic chains containing atoms of oxygen or nitrogen. The difunctional molecules themselves contained two reactive groups which could easily be linked to chains of more than a hundred molecular units. The superpolymers discovered by Carothers could be essentially divided into two classes: the polyesters (containing oxygen) and the polyamides (containing nitrogen).

In 1934, seeking to form polymers of the linear type, Carothers limited his research to the polyamides. In so doing he obtained a new superpolymer very much superior to the first, since it was just as ductile without being soluble in water or subject to destruction by heat. The new substance looked exactly like natural silk and had the same properties. Carothers now stuck closer to his laboratory than the happy prospector to his newly found lode of gold. He pressed forward with energy and feverish curiosity from this second discovery. From the polyamides he devised approximately a hundred different superpolymers.

Naturally enough, excitement reigned in the offices of the Du Pont management when word came of these miracles. At the beginning of 1935 the specimen labeled No. 66 was selected for practical study by another team, and a short while later a pilot plant was built to test the manufacture of No. 66 on a commercial scale. The number 66 came from Carothers's habit of characterizing the superpolymers by the number of atoms of carbon contained in the diacids and the diamines.

But there was still a long way to go from laboratory discovery to the commercial production of the new material. A team of 230 technologists — engineers, chemists, electrical experts, statisticians — were given the task of commercializing Carothers's discovery. Crawford H. Greenewalt is credited with playing the decisive role in this operation. At last, in September, 1938, the big moment arrived and Du Pont announced their new product, nylon. The first nylon plant, built at Seaford, Delaware, had an annual capacity of 4 million pounds. This was to be rapidly doubled even while another plant was being constructed in Martinsville, Virginia. Du Pont is now equipped to turn out around 300 million pounds of nylon a year, but no longer has a manufacturing monopoly. Six other chemical companies compete with the Wilmington firm in nylon manufacture, whether of nylon 66 or a different type. Getting Carothers's discovery into production cost a fortune, but Du Pont has been fabulously rewarded.

And what did Carothers get out of his invention? Painfully sensitive and becoming more and more unstable, he began to drink with alarming frenzy. The list is long of creators unable to face up to their creations. He did not live to see the subsequent success of his discovery — friends say he always carried a vial of cyanide in his pocket.

How did superpolymer 66 come to be named nylon? The director of the Nylon Department at Rhodiaceta, in Lyons, France, told me that a poll was taken among Du Pont employees to find a name for this fantastic new fiber. Nylon was chosen because it signified nothing, was euphonious and easy to pronounce in all languages.

The Second World War did not have as extraordinary an effect on Du Pont fortunes as did the First. The Wilmington firm, to be sure, was the largest producer of explosives in the United States — and still is among the largest in the world. However, by the time of this war, Du Pont explosives constituted only one division of its innumerable activities. Even though from 1940 to 1946 Du Pont made a record tonnage of explosives (America produced 20 per cent more than during World War I), it seems clearly to be the case that Du Pont's direct participation in defense production as such was less than that of several other big American corporations.

All industry became the "arsenal of democracy" after 1941. Beginning in 1940, true enough, Du Pont helped England measure up to total war. But this conflict demanded more cars, trucks, uniforms, food supplies and planes than gunpowder and dynamite. Following Pearl Harbor, President Roosevelt mobilized the American economy on a wartime basis. There was no longer any question of merely soliciting industry's participation in national defense. Meanwhile capitalism had undergone an evolution. Even in America the idea of allowing industrialists to make huge profits from their war production would no longer have been tolerated. A system became generalized whereby defense orders were filled only at a very much reduced profit controlled by the government. More than this, businessmen of greatest prominence accepted high positions of public responsibility as "dollar-a-year men."

Those interested in statistics can take a look at some figures published by Du Pont: Over and beyond all its orders for explosives, the company contributed to national defense enough nylon to make 3,860,275 parachutes, nylon plies for 540,650 bomber tires, enough dye for 10 million uniforms, enough Lucite for transparent cockpit domes on 370,000 planes, 50,929 miles of movie film, enough cellophane to form a ribbon 11.3 feet wide stretching from the earth to the moon. . . .

It then came about that a group of scientists, among them a number of European Jews fleeing from Nazi persecution, brought to a head theories out of which evolved the most fantastic means of destruction the world had ever known. The American government needed technologists able to translate this theory into practice. It was for this reason that one of Du Pont's most brilliant chemists, Crawford H. Greenewalt, was visited by a mysterious envoy who took him away to observe Enrico Fermi's first chain reaction. Some months later, one after another, Greenewalt's best assistants began to disappear, and all that their families and friends knew of their whereabouts was that they were working on Project TNX. At the end of 1942, TNX gave birth to the Manhattan Project, which was placed under the direction of General Leslie Groves. The task at hand was to perfect processes for the manufacture of plutonium. The objective was the atom bomb, which was to be assembled at Los Alamos.

Two Du Pont technicians, E. B. Yancey and Roger Williams, were assigned the job of constructing the Hanford plant, where the plutonium would be produced, in the state of Washington, not far from the Grand Coulee Dam. As for Mr. Greenewalt, his job was to coordinate the work of the technologists. Today at Wilmington they insist that the Du Pont Company was only indirectly involved in the making of the Hiroshima bomb. After the war, and up to 1957, Du Pont was managing two Atomic Energy Commission plants. But today it manages only one, Savannah River, whose main product is said to be nuclear fuel for peaceful uses.

The super power of the United States enabling it to build the atom bomb came from the colossal organized power of the "big companies." Would it not seem logical for the government to encourage, for the physical safety of America, the continuance of these individual giants instead of breaking them up?

In 1933 chemists working in England for Imperial Chemical Industries Ltd. had forced the copolymerization of liquid ethylene and aldehyde under extremely high pressure. In this way they obtained for the first time a plastic resulting from the polymerization of ethylene. The event had passed almost unnoticed. Without saying a word to anyone, Imperial Chemical went ahead with research leading to the eventual manufacture of plastic materials based on this process. The war came, and with it the recognition of the advantages of polyethylenes for insulating material being sought by the British government for radar. Forthwith a plant was built in England for the mass production of this substance. Meanwhile Sir Harry Gowan, president of ICI, wrote to his "excellent friend," Walter S. Carpenter, Jr., then president of Du Pont, to let him know what was happening — it was September, 1941 — and to advise him to make arrangements as soon as possible to use the ICI patent in the United States. All this was perfectly natural, for since 1907 Du Pont and ICI had had cooperation agreements. Three Wilmington technologists flew to London and returned with information supplied by Sir Harry. The U.S. Navy then financed the construction of a plant for Du Pont at Belle in West Virginia; but in December, 1942, the Navy, feeling that Du Pont was dragging its feet, transferred the order to Union Carbide. This latter company supplied the government its first polyethylene plastic for use in radar. After the war Du Pont prohibited Union Carbide from continuing to manufacture this product without a licensing agreement, reclaiming its place as the sole representative of ICI in the United States. Such an agreement was signed on the basis of a $500,000 cash payment, plus a 5 per cent royalty on everything made by Union Carbide. American public opinion was aroused by this arrangement. President Truman assigned the Department of Justice the job of breaking Du Pont–Imperial Chemical ties on the grounds that they ran contrary to the antitrust law. In June, 1952, Judge Sylvester Ryan handed down a decision which ordered Du Pont to yield its license to make polyethylene to all companies capable of making use of the process. Since 1953, Eastman Kodak, Dow Chemical, National Distillers, Spencer Chemical and Monsanto have joined Union Carbide in competition with Du Pont. Superabundance succeeded rarity. For several years the United States capacity for producing polyethylene plastics has outstripped the need, and export has become difficult, since foreign countries — Canada, France and Italy, not to mention England — have been selling them at equivalent or lower prices.

Although Du Pont still maintains today a leading place among American powder and explosives manufacturers, it appears that Du Pont is not interested in getting into the production of scientific weapons such as missiles and rockets.* The company is functioning outside the field of national defense, though continuing with explosives and high-energy substances for carbureting gases needed for rockets and missiles. Remington Arms, now a Du Pont subsidiary, still makes conventional arms, such as rifles (with nylon stocks) and

---

* Recently, however, a research branch of Du Pont has been working on high-energy fuels for missiles.

automatic weapons. Military and sporting powders still show good sales, as do the explosives used in mines, quarries, the petroleum industry, road-building, and the demolition and construction of buildings. One of these explosives, TNT (trinitrotoluene), has recently received publicity in an unusual way: the power of nuclear and thermo-nuclear bombs is measured in equivalents (expressed in kilotons or megatons) of TNT. Hence, while this does not pretend to be a technical book, it may be mentioned in passing that TNT is prepared by the nitration of a common industrial solvent, toluene, added to a mixture of sulfuric and nitric acids. The resulting product is, according to technicians, "used to a limited extent in blasting agents to produce especially strong grades." Despite its activities in this supposedly dangerous field, Du Pont maintains one of the best safety records in American industry.

At the end of 1961 Du Pont ranked eighth among the 100 largest U.S. non-financial corporations; its operating investment amounted to $3,134,000,000, and there were 226,900 stockholders, among whom were 51,000 of the 88,000 company employees.

During the past 25 years, Du Pont's sales have grown yearly at a rate of almost 9 per cent. For more than 35 years, Du Pont has been able to finance its capital-expenditure requirements from internal sources and has been debt-free since 1925. Very few big American companies are in the same situation. It is of interest to note that the profit margin, which was 18.9 per cent of the net operating investment in 1939, never reached such a high in the following years. It was at its lowest point in 1944 with 7 per cent and in 1960 it was only 11.6 per cent.

Subsidiary companies of Du Pont, some of them in existence for years, others just created, have plants in Argentina, Brazil, Chile, Mexico, Venezuela and Canada, as well as in Europe. Du Pont has also set up an operation in Japan in cooperation with Japanese chemical companies such as Showa Denko.

By far the largest foreign Du Pont investment is the one in Canada. Out of a total of 280 million dollars invested abroad, it represents 135 million dollars, as against 60 million for Europe and 85 million for Latin America. Du Pont of Canada has its headquarters in Montreal and its research center in Kingston, Ontario, as well as plants for the manufacture of polyethylene, cellophane, nylon filaments, Orlon staples, explosives and lacquers at Maitland, Shawinigan, Kingston, Ajax, Sarnia, Whitby and North Bay. It is controlled by E. I. Du Pont de Nemours of Wilmington (with 81.5 per cent of the common stock), but this does not prevent it from being Canadian — from employing Canadians almost exclusively and from having only a few Americans on its administrative council.

Du Pont of Canada goes back only to 1954. Actually,

however, its origin dates back much further — 1954 merely marks the year when it grew out of Canadian Explosives Ltd., founded in 1910 to seal the alliance between Du Pont de Nemours and Nobel Ltd. Its origin might be traced back even further to 1877, to one of the firms, Hamilton Powder Company (successor of Canada Powder Company, founded in 1852), which Lammot du Pont through merger brought under the control of the Wilmington powder-makers. The sales of Du Pont of Canada Ltd. in 1954 were 55.7 million dollars. They reached almost 100 million dollars in 1960. But in Canada, as in the United States, the profit margin has been lower every year since 1956, with the exception of 1959.

In Europe there are 100 per cent Du Pont affiliates in Holland, Great Britain, Belgium, Switzerland and France. An application for approval to form a joint Spanish company has been filed with the Spanish government by Du Pont Energia e Industrias Aragonesas. Beyond this, Du Pont also has a 26 per cent interest in a German firm, Pigment Chemie, using certain of its patents. Early in 1960 a large Du Pont plant manufacturing neoprene opened its doors in Northern Ireland. A Du Pont paint plant in Belgium and an Orlon plant in Holland are now in operation. This Dutch affiliate has under construction another plant, costing several million dollars, to make plastics for the European Common Market. It is very clear that this Common Market has a special interest for the American Du Pont de Nemours. E. I. Du Pont de Nemours International (S.A.), installed in Geneva, Switzerland, for good political, geographical and fiscal reasons, is responsible for sales, technical service and market analysis for a wide range of Du Pont products all over Europe. Du Pont expects to have an increasingly improved position among large enterprises of the international class through its exports and manufactures under license. And by virtue of its foreign manufacturing (over 400 million dollars' worth of business), Du Pont counts, and will count even more, as one of the most important American corporations operating outside the United States.

11

Inside the Family

Car, estans ainsi tous parens et
alliez l'ung l'aultre nous trou-
vasmes que personne n'etait
d'iceulx ne pere ne mere, frere
ne soeur, oncle ne tante, cousin
ne nepveu, gendre ne brus,
parrain ne marraisne de
l'aultre.

RABELAIS
Pantagruel IV, 9

O<small>N</small> D<small>ECEMBER</small> 21, 1949, under a headline reading:
"Du Pont Empire Heirs to Mark Fabulous Era;
Family Reached America on Icy Tub in 1800," the Chi-
cago *Tribune* announced festivities planned by the du
Ponts to mark the 150th anniversary of their arrival at
Newport. On January 19, 1950, more than 600 du Ponts
attended this extraordinary reunion, among them Eng-
lish, French and Swiss members of the family — the
Meuniers, Dombres, Martins, Mottus, Huebers, de
Tregomains, and others — as well as some Italian mem-
bers, the Silvestro Bassutis.

[237]

A large formal dinner was served at Longwood, Pierre's estate, with all the guests seated at small tables. Overseen by Newman of Holland & Co., caterers by appointment for the company's banquets since 1900, the menu included johnnycake, ragoût of terrapin, filets mignon and game pies weighing 35 pounds apiece, all to be washed down by claret and champagne. During the dinner an organist played on the big pipe organ in the conservatory.

Most of the du Ponts knew each other. However, in a reunion of this dimension, with some of the guests coming from great distances, identification could be difficult, and for this reason everyone was provided with a badge with his name on it before taking his place at the tables. The color of the badges varied according to the branch of origin. It was characteristic of the family that order and organization reigned, and characteristic too, that economy was considered. The dinner was not free. The price paid was 50 cents for each year of the guest's life. Thus the youngest paid only $8, while the patriarch of the group, Pierre Samuel, who had just turned eighty, paid the maximum price of $40.

Those who attended have a vivid memory of this astonishing reunion. One in-law reported:

Festivities actually got under way on December 31. I was newly married and this evening was for me the first time I was closely involved in a family ceremony. They had decided against taking the big ballroom of the Hotel Du Pont on New Year's Eve, since each year at this time it was traditionally given over to company employees. Since no other large rooms were available, they all gathered at Granogue, Irénée's home. Granogue is not a small place, but certainly nothing like a Newport Mansion. Not big enough to take care of so many people. First formality was to present oneself to Irénée, who did the receiving at the head of the stairs — there was a mob. Immediately ahead of my wife and me there was a gentleman who, shaking Irénée's hand, introduced himself as "William Shakespeare." Without cracking a smile, Irénée bade him welcome. From this I got the impression that the du Ponts, when among themselves, liked to make jokes, and I was tempted to say to the dean of the family, who had never met me before: "I'm Napoleon and my wife is Josephine." Fortunately I didn't do this, for later, at the Longwood reunion dinner, it happened that this same Shakespeare of December 31 sat at our table. He assured us that that was indeed his real name. He, too, had married a du Pont. Another neighbor at the same table, who hadn't caught the explanation, was visibly impressed. During the dinner she said to me: "I knew we were a very old family but I didn't realize we went all the way back to Shakespeare!"

The European members of the family had arrived in time to take part in the New Year's celebration, which was arranged exactly as in past years and which each year reaffirms du Pont ties. It is a family day which commemorates their arrival in Newport on New Year's Eve, 1799, when they numbered only thirteen. For New Year's Day "calling," all male du Ponts "old enough to dress themselves" put on their best bib and tucker (the older gentlemen have given up tails, but still wear striped pants and morning jackets) to pay their respects to the ladies. The ritual begins in the morning on the stroke of nine, and quite often several men of the same branch make their calls in one car. For sentimental reasons, they use the oldest vehicles owned by the family, some of them museum pieces such as the Du Pont car in which Mrs. E. Paul du Pont is driven every January 1 to join her family group — an eight-cylinder phaeton made by her late husband's company in 1928. Also, there is Mrs. Philip du Pont's 1927 Rolls-Royce, which is seldom taken out of the garage except on this occasion. The New Year's Day itinerary for the men is not completed until late in the afternoon, since there is a long list of calls and stops must be made at every house. It would be impossible to cover this territory were it not telescoped by grouping all the womenfolk and children of the same branch, married and unmarried, under one roof and rotating each year. In 1959 the circuit was reduced in this fashion to only thirteen points of call.

Miss Aileen du Pont, who has become the guardian of family tradition, explained to me that on New Year's Day her own branch unfailingly serve "a gigantesque pâté" sufficient for at least seventy-five persons. In fact, it seems that "Miss Aileen" makes this herself. The story goes that the recipe has been passed down in the family from Victor's wife, whose idea it was in the first place to bring along the big pâté which helped save them from starving on that adventurous crossing in 1799.

However, this round of New Year's Day "calling" is only half of the obligation laid on the du Pont gentlemen. Each lady, young and old, must receive a present from each and every caller. There is annually prepared — in recent years by Mr. William Winder Laird — a list of family recipients which is coordinated with the itinerary and specifies who and how many and where. Thus the number of gifts to be taken into each house is organized in advance.

The du Ponts have a rule that these gifts shall be only tokens of affection. Generally each caller takes gifts all of one kind — it might be boxes of cookies, candies, fancy matches, little jars of this and that to eat. When Pierre Samuel was alive he brought such gifts as beautiful bunches of grapes from his own hothouse. The family spirit is thus expressed without any fear that it might lead to prodigality. From this custom one might conclude that the family still shows marks of its Protestant French origins which stemmed in part from the city of Lyons and from Switzerland. (The Lyonnais have the reputation of liking to squeeze a penny. Their neighbors, the Swiss, are supposed to be even more economical. The French have an expression "drinking like a Swiss" to describe someone sitting by himself at a café table, presumably for fear of having to pick up the tab for someone else.)

How many of the du Ponts speak French? On the male side no more than the average among Americans educated at private schools and colleges. On the female side the proportion is greater and increasing among the young, not because they are du Ponts but because the young ones of the family are at last beginning to travel.

Benjamin Franklin wrote to a friend on October 2, 1770: "I could take with me to America Messieurs du Pont, or some other French friends with their good ladies. I might then, by mixing them with my friends in Philadelphia, form a little happy society that would prevent my ever wishing to again visit Europe." Over the years, the home-loving du Ponts have held this same opinion and have formed among themselves their own little happy society.

Some du Ponts have not forgotten their French roots. At Chevannes, near Nemours, a spot to which the du Ponts are connected through the ancestral Pierre-Samuel, the inhabitants catch an occasional glimpse of some one of the family coming to look around. For the rare visitor to this agglomeration of perhaps thirty houses clustered around an ivy-choked church tower, Chevannes is nothing more than a little village in the province of Gâtinais. But for the du Ponts, it is a place of pilgrimage. Pushing open the gate of the ancient graveyard in front of the church, I noticed, at the base of the belfry tower, a simple grave, that of Pierre-Samuel's first wife, Nicole, ancestor of all the American du Ponts. On a marble plaque made in 1907 — a copy of the original stone destroyed by time — I read the epitaph composed in 1785 by the grieving Physiocrat:

HERE LIES THE BODY

OF

NOBLE, ECONOMICAL AND GENEROUS DAME
MADAME NICOLE-CHARLOTTE-MARIE-LOUISE LE DÉE,
WIFE OF MESSIRE PIERRE-SAMUEL DU PONT
CHEVALIER OF THE ROYAL ORDER OF VASA
BORN AT VIRE
DIED AT BOIS-DES-FOSSÉS
SEPTEMBER 3, 1784
AT THE AGE OF 41 YEARS, 3 MONTHS AND 28 DAYS.
SHE HAS BEEN THE CONSTANT HAPPINESS OF HER
HUSBAND AND HER CHILDREN.
SHE HAS BEEN THE EXAMPLE OF HONOUR TO HER
PARENTS AND HER FRIENDS, THE CONSOLATION,
THE BLESSING, THE NEVER-ENDING HELP TO THE
POOR OF THE PARISH.
SHE IS NO DOUBT IN HEAVEN.

This old burial ground by the church has been left in untended naturalness, the only adornment a sturdy growth of tall, half-flowering weeds.

The church, which dates from the fifteenth century,

is not entirely abandoned, but has no permanently assigned priest. A notice nailed to the closed door announces that masses are still celebrated four or five times a year. "If you want the key to go in," the proprietor of the village store said, "all you have to do is ask the blacksmith." This I did, but the blacksmith happened to be far out in his fields. Two hours later, I entered the church and read an inscription on a pillar, that the church had been "restored in 1930 thanks to the generosity of Mr. Pierre-Samuel du Pont de Nemours, resident of Wilmington, United States, Delaward [*sic*]." Another plaque recalls the memory of "Philippe Nicolas Harmand, former mayor of Chevannes," to whom the Physiocrat wrote his last letter in France before striking out on his American venture and who had brought the Physiocrat his food while he was in hiding at the Institute in Paris. Harmand bought Bois-des-Fossés when the du Ponts pulled up their stakes.

Needless to say, I did not leave the village of Chevannes without finding out what had become of Bois-des-Fossés. When I inquired of the village storekeeper whether there was a property in that area by the name of Bois-des-Fossés, she told me: "The Château? Of course! But the old house is gone now. Follow the road as far as the little bridge that crosses the brook and take the road to the right. It's not far from there. You'll see the farm and pretty soon the iron gate of the property."

She was right, there was practically nothing left of the original house of Messire Pierre-Samuel du Pont. The eighteenth-century dwelling, which had had a story added to it in 1825, had been torn down. An interim owner, an industrialist with no respect for things of the past, had built in its stead a mediocre house without style or character, except what comes from bourgeois comfort. Only the farm outbuildings remain, probably very much the same as they were in the days of the Physiocrat. As with all farms in Beauce and Gâtinais, they give onto a courtyard from within a closed wall. Hereabouts it is never the main house which gives an idea of the importance of the estate, but the farm buildings. The cowbarn, sheepfold and stable reveal by their dimensions how many acres there are to till and fertilize. At Bois-des-Fossés the working buildings have become too big for the land, which, piece by piece, has been sold off to different buyers. Today the actual estate comprises, I believe, no more than a hundred acres or so. It is reported that the du Ponts recently took over some responsibility for the maintenance of this old property. There still remains the form of an elegant but small French garden as well as the rather run-down structure which to this day has kept the pretentious name of the "Orangerie," both of which do date back to du Pont times. It is from the tangled tall woods on the other side that Bois-des-Fossés got its name.

The straight drive bordered by apple trees that runs

from the "Château's" iron gate to the highway is the very one followed by Pierre-Samuel when, on June 20, 1794, he was taken away under guard as the prisoner of red-bonneted patriots, on a walk which, but for incredible luck, could have been the road to eternity for him.

It is certainly a temptation to generalize on the du Ponts, on their tastes, their way of living, their habits. If the estimates of the company's public relations department are correct, there were in 1957 more than 1200 du Ponts — 900 in the United States — and each year about 34 more are born. By the year 2000, the number may conceivably reach 2600.

If it is said that this group, because of the numerous intermarriages, represents something approaching a "race," it can also be said, as has Eugene Pittard, that "human biology is a different sort of complex than yeast." The proper thing, then, is to avoid looking for easily discernible characteristics common to all du Ponts. All that can be done in this general regard is to try to identify the traits common to the du Ponts who have a major interest in the enterprise that bears their name, and who today live in Wilmington or its environs. As a rule, the ones selected at Du Pont to be conservators of the corporation's familial aspect come from among this group or their relatives. It is fair to add that if there is solidarity among the top-ranking du Ponts, lesser ones share it, too.

It seems to me that no people, no family or man can be understood until one has seen their graves. Anyone born a du Pont, married to a du Pont — in Wilmington, as in Spain, *"la cuisse anoblit,"* or, literally, "the thigh ennobles" — or who is even divorced from a du Pont, provided he has never remarried, has a right to be buried in their family cemetery. This exclusive place of repose is located on a hill called Sand Hole, because from it, long ago, sand was taken to make mortar for the mills along the Brandywine. A low wall encloses the cemetery on the valley side, an iron fence on the side of the estates where the du Ponts live. Trees — any number of beautiful trees — shade the simple gravestones, most of which have no cross or religious symbol. Wild grass invades the paths, moss grows on the stones. Can one speak of disorder in this garden of the dead? No, it is certainly not that. . . . There is an order of sorts here, the order of Nature, with birds and squirrels and rabbits. At the oldest stone of all, where bees sipped the honeysuckle covering the half-obliterated inscription, I found the grave of the Physiocrat friend of Rousseau, Turgot, Necker, Bernardin de Saint-Pierre, Lavoisier and Lafayette. Pantheism, *"bon sauvage,"* thatched cottage, human kindness, Nature, Supreme Being . . . all of these ideals from the romantic eighteenth century are reflected in the simplicity of his burial place.

SACRED TO THE MEMORY OF
PIERRE SAMUEL DU PONT DE NEMOURS
KNIGHT OF THE ORDER OF VASA
OF THE LEGION OF HONOR AND OF THE ORDER OF
THE LIS
COUNSELLOR OF STATE
MEMBER OF THE FIRST CONSTITUENT ASSEMBLY
PRESIDENT OF THE COUNCIL OF ANCIENTS
MEMBER OF THE INSTITUTE OF FRANCE
BORN IN PARIS DECEMBER A.D. 1739
DIED AT THE ELEUTHERIAN MILLS
AUGUST 17 A.D. 1817

Only one monument, a not too imposing obelisk, dominates the line of gravestones running to the right from Pierre-Samuel, the line belonging to the older branch; those on the left belong to the younger one. The obelisk was erected in memory of Admiral Samuel Francis du Pont, Victor's son. Hidden among the trees, a broken column symbolizes the hazards of the calling that enriched the du Ponts, and beneath this column lies Lammot, killed in an explosion. Lammot was the grandson of Eleuthère-Irénée, founder of the powder works and father of the three brothers — Pierre, Irénée, Lammot — who did most to shape the business into the form persisting to this day. Farther away, an inscription carved in relief on one oval gravestone reads: BONTÉ, BEAUTÉ, PURETÉ, GRÂCE, GAIETÉ, TENDRESSE, ENTENDE-

MENT, BIENFAISANCE, PUISSANT AMOUR, RADIANT ESPRIT,
GRANDEUR. PASSANT, INCLINE-TOI.* (Kindness, Beauty,
Purity, Grace, Gaiety, Tenderness, Understanding,
Benevolence, Powerful Love, Radiant Spirit, Nobility
. . . Passerby, Bow Thy Head.)

Finally, near the wall under leafy bushes, I discovered the grave of "Francois-Joseph Jandelle, born at
Pusey, Departement de la Haute-Saone, April 13, 1782.
. . . Emigrated to the U.S.A. with E. I. Du Pont de
Nemours, Sept. 1799. Died August 17, 1856." Unlike his
master, this servant who emigrated from France at the
age of seventeen did not make a great fortune in America. But if the numerous Jeandells of Wilmington are
his descendants, he too left his mark.

This cemetery brought memories of a graveyard in
Nauvoo, Illinois. Also romantic, also close to nature, also
a place where Frenchmen sleep. I was suddenly struck
by the strange affinity between the two. In both places
lie Frenchmen who left in search of an ideal born of the
eighteenth century. Those of Wilmington buried around
the revolutionary Physiocrat had succeeded in establishing themselves in American society under the stand-

---

* This inscription in French was composed by the inconsolable
widower of a du Pont. I was told by a New York Theosophist that up
to his death he came daily to lay white roses on this grave, and that,
being a spiritualist, he believed he was in communication with his
wife. He was convinced that when his spirit was in touch with hers
in the infinite the white roses would turn pink. He also had the table
set at home as if she had just gone out and would be back for
dinner. I was assured that even after he had remarried, he did not
in the least change this singular habit.

ard of a community capitalism. The Mormons had already come and gone from Nauvoo when these Frenchmen arrived there in 1848 with Etienne Cabet. They had gone to organize for themselves a communist society of "Icariens," but they misconceived the political direction of America. Theirs was a Utopian dream born of the same ideals that inspired the Physiocrat but unlike his, doomed to die.

Delaware is the 49th state in size. In population it is 46th, with 440,000 inhabitants. The city of Wilmington, near which Eleuthère-Irénée set up his powder mill, is just about midway between New York and Washington. Through it passes the railroad linking the national capital to the largest city in the United States. Past Wilmington, too, flows the uninterrupted stream of cars, nine million of them a year, coming from the New Jersey Turnpike, the great superhighway which ends at the Delaware Memorial Bridge. Extending two miles over the Delaware River, the bridge connects with Route 13. It was Coleman who had State Highway 13 constructed at his own expense, and who is credited with this historic comment: "I am going to build a monument a hundred miles high and lay it down on the ground." A monument to his glory — and his ambition — and over it he later marched, as it were, to the Senate seat he had so deeply craved.

It was the English explorer Henry Hudson, then in

the service of the Dutch East India Company, who first reconnoitered the Delaware River in 1609. He named it in honor of Lord De La Warr, governor of Virginia, who himself never laid eyes on the stream. A Dutch settlement and fort were built at a place called Zwaanendael. Two years later, the first settlers having either fled or been massacred, a band of Swedish whalers arrived at the Delaware and ambitiously named the settlement New Sweden. This settlement was located where a part of the city of Wilmington is found today. Three things have survived from the Swedes' brief stay: the name of Christina (later to be assumed by the Christiana Securities, with an added *a*) which these people gave to a tributary of the Delaware in honor of their queen, daughter of Gustavus Adolphus; a Lutheran church which calls itself Swedish but whose membership ceased to be Swedish years ago; and finally the Rocks, shown to tourists as the mooring site of the first Swedish boats. We know from records of the period that only 98 persons were left in the colony by 1644. Twenty years later there were even fewer. In consequence, not the least protest was evoked when the English governor of New York, in 1664, extended his jurisdiction to New Sweden. Around 1730 a Pennsylvania Quaker, Thomas Willing, who had married Catherine Justis, a Swedish settler, founded Willingtown. A second Quaker, William Shipley, bought several tracts of land and built a market place which attracted a colony of Quakers. In

1739 this became the Wilmington which today, with its 100,000 inhabitants, is the largest city in Delaware. It is not a picturesque place, since few streets have kept the colonial atmosphere which has been retained in Dover and New Castle, where once a year on Dover Day or New Castle Day the houses are opened for the admiration of the modern world.

D. B. Warden, former American consul in Paris, in 1820 wrote the following geographical description of the state:

The highest chain of hill on the peninsula formed by Delaware and Chesapeake Bays crosses the state from north to south and the numerous streams arising from its breasts flow from east to west. At its midpoint this chain is 15 miles from the Delaware River. Situated two miles east of this river, Wilmington is only 100 feet above tidewater. The Brandywine, which arises in Pennsylvania, runs 40 miles before emptying into the Delaware. It is navigable up to Wilmington for boats drawing no more than 8 feet. The Christina arises in the state of Maryland and joins the Brandywine a mile above its confluence with the Delaware. . . .

On touring the countryside around Wilmington, one sees new châteaux and imposing houses which give a good idea of the importance of the du Pont fortune. Most of these du Pont estates are of recent origin, and all appear to be in constant use. The du Ponts really live here. They have preserved their ties to the state (not forgetting taxes are favorable). A few have crossed the line into Pennsylvania to build their houses, but still they hover on the very edge of Delaware. The close-knit du Pont family exists as it is today because of the enduring presence of the Du Pont Company. Thus far, these great and beautiful properties have avoided the fate of the former mansions of the Carnegies, Vanderbilts, Goulds, Fricks, Dukes, Morgans, and Astors, which have been torn down or institutionalized.

Very few of the family live in the city of Wilmington proper, most preferring country life. However, in the city there are a few sections with attractive old houses, some of which belong to families that occasionally speak of the du Ponts as newcomers. These people are the descendants of the Tatnall, Rodney, Bush, Layton, Gray, Draper, Ridgeley, Canby, Janvier, Sellers, Holcombe and Townsend families, to mention only some who were in Wilmington before the advent of the du Ponts. Many large new houses with well-tended lawns bordering the parks are owned by Du Pont Company executives who either earn comfortable salaries or are now on company pension.

The Negro sections are teeming with children, yet do not have the appearance of dilapidated misery as in Harlem or the Negro sections of other big cities. Wilmington is not far from the Mason-Dixon line, laid down between 1763 and 1767 to mark the boundary between colonial Pennsylvania and Maryland. In Delaware, an agricultural enterprise is called a "farm," whereas the term "plantation," with its slaveholding connotations, is used in the neighboring state of Maryland. French Street, named to honor the memory of French *émigrés,** King Street, with its shopfronts where appetizing chickens, fruits and vegetables are on display, strict policemen, a disciplined populace. We must remember that even though the whipping post was never much used, it was not officially abolished in Delaware until after World War II.

One sees, next to a number of bank and corporation buildings, the two squat and most imposing buildings of the city: the Du Pont Building, linked by an overpass to the De Nemours Building. At the right there is a public square in front of which a gentleman in a three-cornered hat (not a du Pont, but Caesar Rodney) sits on his bronze horse as if still galloping to Philadelphia to cast that deciding vote for Independence. Thereafter the courthouse, the public library, the post office and a red brick Protestant church with a white belfry. Such is Wilmington, a fief of the du Ponts. And more than this, titular headquarters for a number of other big American corporations.

More than 20,000 American corporations and many

---

* It appears that most of these *émigrés* were not lacking in means. They entertained one another and introduced ideas from the greater world among the astonished farmers and shopkeepers of the town. At the corner of Tatnall Street, there was a pond filled with frogs. These Messieurs taught the villagers how to cook them so as to make a savory dish. The youngsters went fishing for frogs, and sold the legs to customers, they being in great demand, according to Elizabeth Montgomery, author of *Reminiscences of Wilmington.*

foreign ones as well have their titular headquarters in Delaware, since in this state the legal formalities of incorporation are most simply, most rapidly and least expensively accomplished. Also, the laws regulating corporations, once they are established, are least meddlesome. Of the 1149 corporations listed on the New York Stock Exchange in January, 1961, the legal address of 400 was Delaware, of 147 New York, 91 New Jersey, 69 Pennsylvania. Among the biggest and best known of the Delaware "400" are Coca-Cola, Allis-Chalmers, Wrigley, General Motors, Ford Motor Co., Bethlehem Steel, American Viscose, Sears Roebuck, Getty Oil, National Steel and Burlington Industries. The basic law regulating corporations in Delaware goes back to 1899. By coincidence, no doubt, 1899 was also the year when Colonel Henry Algernon du Pont decided it was necessary (see Chapter 6) to incorporate the E. I. Du Pont de Nemours Company in Wilmington. The original statute has been modified, through the years, only in a few details. This has led Chancellor Collins J. Seitz of the Delaware Court of Chancery to write: "Our corporative laws date back some 60 years. They are clear and no less clear is the jurisprudence which permits them to be interpreted before the courts in case of litigation." A businessman gave me this supplementary gloss: "If a corporation issues a million shares of common stock at $100 a share in the state of New York, right away he must pay a tax of $50,000. In

Delaware he would get away with only $2650." It was a Delaware attorney by the name of Josiah Marvel who headed the group of lawyers charged with drawing up the statute in 1899. It was specified at this time that out-of-state corporations could be legally represented by an agent. Josiah Marvel was the first to make a killing from this clause, by offering to represent a number of corporations through his Corporation Service Co. At once he found a great many clients, who paid him on a sliding scale according to services rendered.

This ingenious businessman is no longer among the living. And gone too is his successor, but the Corporation Service Co. exists, even though meanwhile it has lost much of its earlier importance. It is controlled by the heirs of Josiah Marvel and has offices in the Delaware Trust Building (headquarters, it will be recalled, of the Delaware Trust Company founded by Alfred du Pont during the family war). Among its more recently established and flourishing competitors in Wilmington are the Corporation Trust Co., the Corporation Guaranty & Trust, and the U. S. Corporation Co. For these incorporation firms, once the formalities of actual incorporation are completed, work consists mainly of printing certificates, proxies, circulars, reports of meetings and the like for the companies represented. The publishing house of Prentice-Hall has an office in the Delaware Trust Building to catch this business. Up to recent times, the principal difficulty experienced by these corporative agents was to make sure — as required by the 1899 law — that the names of the firms which they served as correspondents were duly inscribed on a gigantic directory in the lobby of their building. One of these directory boards alone had more than 10,000 names. Now this aspect of the law has been happily amended and the lobby directories have disappeared. It might be noted that Wilmington corporative agents are very discreet and prefer that the list of firms which they represent shall remain confidential. No less discreet, it seems, are the stockholders of the big corporations who attend the annual meetings in Delaware localities. Seldom do more than a handful take the trouble to show up. This facilitates the work of the board members, since they need not waste time answering questions which might otherwise be asked them. Only the Hotel Du Pont might complain about this arrangement, on grounds of lack of patronage; but in fact it is always filled, thanks to the comings and goings of people doing business with the Du Pont Company. Needless to say, E. I. Du Pont de Nemours & Co. does not have to have anyone representing it in Wilmington, since it has been resident there for more than a century.

The company owns the twin Du Pont and Nemours Buildings. In the former is located the Hotel Du Pont with its shops, bars, ballroom, a large cafeteria and a restaurant, and the recently modernized lobby, with its paneled plaster ceiling, which serves as a point of as-

sembly both for residents of the city and the people
passing through, while the basement cafeteria is the
meeting place of company employees out for a coffee
break. (At Du Pont, everyone is regularly at work by
eight in the morning.) There is a theater on the ground
floor of the same building and there plays are occasionally tried out before going to Broadway. In attendance
at these performances can be seen everybody who
counts in Wilmington's limited social circle.

Need we say that the two local dailies, a morning and
an afternoon paper, are indirectly controlled by some
members of the du Pont family, their stock being almost entirely owned by Christiana Securities? One of
these newspapers owns Wilmington's main radio station.

Need we add that 25,000 people from Wilmington
and vicinity are directly employed by Du Pont? And to
give some idea of the family name in the area, in the
Wilmington phone book appear the names of over 40
different du Ponts, not to mention 43 different branches
of the company, as well as the Du Pont foundations,
hospitals, schools and philanthropic works, the clubs to
which they belong, the airport they have built, as well
as the innumerable du Pont women who bear their
husbands' names, but who are du Ponts nonetheless.

Generally speaking, it is fair to say that if the du
Ponts rule, they rule democratically, and that although

they may be a clan in which intermarriage is as fre-
quent as among European royalty, the du Ponts harbor
no racial, political or religious prejudices. The du Ponts
have proved this. When accused once of being anti-
Semitic, Pierre Samuel promptly retorted: "How could
I be when my mother has Jewish blood, and my wife,
too?" The Jewish strain came, in fact, from the Belins.
A relative by marriage highly regarded among the du
Ponts has Asiatic blood, I was assured, since he is the
son of a Protestant missionary and a young Morro
woman whom the missionary had married when he was
in the Far East.

Pierre Samuel du Pont, who died in 1954, was one of
the greatest among the greats who made the company
what it is. What sort of man was he? The death of his
father, Lammot, by accident when Pierre Samuel was a
boy of thirteen left an indelible mark on him, it appears,
for thereafter he looked on himself as head of the family
of eleven children, of whom he was the oldest. Graduat-
ing in 1890 from the Massachusetts Institute of Technology, where gifted du Ponts are generally enrolled,
he certainly resented the fact that his Uncle Eugene,
president of the company, seemed to pay little attention
to him during his years of company employ between
1891 and 1899. He proved his own value to himself by
his success working with his cousin Coleman before returning to Wilmington with him and Alfred. Taciturn,

reserved, though not to the point that he could have been called either arrogant or timid, this six-footer, in his youth, was a good tennis player and, though he had little liking for social affairs, rarely missed the monthly meetings of the Farmers Club in Philadelphia. There every month he met with friends, successful industrialists for the most part, who were the big landowners of the region. This went on all during the years when he was a bachelor and even later, after he had married one of his cousins. This lady, Alice Belin, was afflicted with deafness but, being highly intelligent, read lips so well that she was able to amuse herself by repeating comments that people had made, as they thought, out of her hearing. Pierre, a man with an esthetic love of music and flowers, bought a 1000-acre property some twelve miles out of Wilmington in Chester County, Pennsylvania, an estate originally given by William Penn to the Quaker George Pierce. There he furnished, not ornately, the Longwood manor and built lovely Italian gardens modeled after those of the Villa Gamberaia, which looks out over the valley of the Arno near Florence. He added fountains and pools with water jets, and immense greenhouses, made both to accommodate the tallest of exotic trees and to shelter the delicate orchids whose unfoldings he watched with passionate interest to the accompaniment of music from a great pipe organ. In his daily life, however, he was a man of simple tastes — he bought his clothes from the local clothier — and there was nothing castle-like about his patioed house; the apartment which he kept at the Carlton House in New York was also relatively modest. But the four spacious rooms which he had reserved for himself in the Empire State Building were rather impressive. Number 8009 is now called the executive suite, but old-timers in the building still refer to it as "Mr. Pierre's suite."

This financial genius became grandiose, even ostentatious, when it came to spending fabulous sums to beautify his park, to build his greenhouses, and in general to design, through these creations, the image of himself that would go down to posterity. The park and greenhouses cost a fortune to keep up — today some forty gardeners are assigned to their maintenance. Once Henry Ford and his wife came to visit at Longwood. The man from Detroit had the habit of calculating the cost of everything he laid eyes on and could not resist the indiscreet impulse to ask his host: "How many men are working for you here?" Pierre's reply was: "Oh, about half of them."

Pierre S. kept a concert artist on monthly stipend just to give organ recitals. However, it appears that it was not Pierre but John J. Raskob, at Archmere, who was the first in Wilmington to indulge in the luxury of having an organ installed. The intimate friendship shared by these two, Raskob the aggressive, Pierre the cautious, was cemented by their many joint activities.

With Pierre's backing, John Raskob amassed the great fortune which was to be inherited by his thirteen children and his widow, who has since married the manager of her Arizona ranch. Up to the end of his life in 1950, he remained Pierre's closest and most influential friend.

Raskob was not the only one who owed much to Pierre S. du Pont. At one point he conceived a great affection for another secretary, a young man by the name of Lewes A. Mason, who died in 1918 from Spanish influenza while in his employ. In his name Pierre founded a 1.2-million-dollar hospital at Westchester, Pennsylvania. An oil painting of Mason occupies, as it always has, the place of honor over the fireplace in Pierre's office at Longwood.

At Longwood he gathered quantities of books into an imposing library. He was very curious about everything to do with his family, and among other treasures succeeded in getting hold of many original historic documents.

The Longwood Library, an independent institution, employing a dozen archivists and secretaries, has received some 10,000 pieces to classify and evaluate so as to make it possible to recount the life of Pierre, in itself a simple fragment, but interesting nonetheless in the long history of the du Ponts. Every facility was put at my disposal for looking through these files. Previously unpublished or little-known material concerning the du Ponts comes in large measure from this source. These dossiers, together with all the documents and volumes collected by Pierre, have been recently removed from Longwood to a new building erected near Hagley to centralize the du Pont archives.

The new Eleutherian Mills Library was dedicated on October 7, 1961, with most of the important family documents on display. It appeared that every adult du Pont had been invited. There were speeches, followed by conducted tours and lunch served under a great tent where family branches gravitated to the same tables. It was fascinating to see this great assembly of uncles, aunts and cousins — so many similar features, similar expressions, and similar actions — all so quiet and Sunday-best, as if the old Physiocrat himself were there.

It was in 1919 that Pierre turned over the presidency of the Du Pont Company to his brother Irénée and took instead the chairmanship of the board, a position which gave him more leisure time. Unfortunately he could not use his free time entirely as he would have liked, since his wealth had become so great that it absorbed a great deal of his energies. For example, having life insurance in the amount of 7.5 million dollars, he did not even have the right to fly in his own plane!

Having no direct heirs, Pierre took precautions during his lifetime to ensure that the enormous capital he had amassed would not be eaten up by taxes, particularly in such fashion as to jeopardize family authority by taking too great a bite out of the common patrimony. It was he who largely endowed the Longwood Foundation in 1937 to maintain his Chester County estate, where the gardens have been open to the public on certain days since 1921. This matter having been taken care of, he transferred his Du Pont and General Motors stock to the Christiana Securities Company and the Delaware Realty Corporation, on condition that he be paid an annual income of $900,000 a year. It is said that these trusts had a hard time scraping up this amount the first year.

His brother Lammot, a man of vigorous temperament, married four times and had five sons and as many daughters. The other brother, Irénée, married his cousin Irene du Pont, and by her had one son and eight daughters. All of Pierre's other brothers and sisters except one were married and had children. This is by far the richest branch of the family today and it is whispered around that anyone who married into this group automatically received one million dollars. This branch is also the most numerously represented on the company's executive committee.

Of the three brothers, Pierre, Lammot and Irénée, who were successively presidents of Du Pont from 1909 to 1940, only one is still alive today: Irénée. He is a sturdy octogenarian* with a still active mind, though

* He was born in December, 1876, and graduated from M.I.T. in 1897.

people who have known him for a long time say that he is "beginning to slow down." He was a vigorous Roosevelt-hater and energetically fought the New Deal, which he thought of as state socialism. Before Prohibition he was a member of the Republican party but got out at the same time as his brother Pierre to join the "repeal movement," since on this one point he went along with Democratic ideas. Smoking his pipe, his spectacles pushed up on his forehead, he seems probably the most remarkable personality in Wilmington. Deservedly respected as the patriarch and dean of the family, he lives on his estate, Granogue, where he has put together an astonishing mineral collection. Until very recently he divided his time between this house and the impressive Xanadu which he built in Cuba. In November, 1961, he received official notice that Castro had nationalized this property for use as a nautical school for boys. Irénée also financed the experiments on the thermal energy of the sea — a subject in which he was deeply interested — made by the French scientist Georges Claude.* It is to Irénée that the company owes its administrative organization, introduced in 1921. This structure had to be only slightly modified when he left his post of honorary chairman in 1959. Until his retirement he showed

---

* Georges Claude died in 1960 at the age of eighty-nine. He was condemned as a collaborator after the liberation of France for having openly supported the Pétain government. It was he who invented the neon light, also liquid air, patents for which are used by Du Pont in their Belle, West Virginia, plant.

up punctually every morning at 7:57 at the Du Pont Building elevator to be carried up to the ninth floor, where his office was located. It was he, it is said, who had an electric clock installed to keep track of the time it took for the elevators to go up and down, in order to silence his colleagues' complaints about the imagined slowness of the service. The organization introduced by Irénée is highly effective and deserves mention in this chapter on the family rather than in the sections on the company as such. It is because of his organization that the du Pont family (who own, according to the highest estimates, only 40 per cent of the stock of E. I. Du Pont de Nemours & Co.) retain control of the business.

As with all corporations, the stockholders meet once a year to hear the annual report and financial statement read and to elect members of the board. The time has passed when the family has all or even a majority of the seats on the board. It is true that by a judicious exercise of democratic principles, they bestow power on those most qualified to wield it. However, key posts seldom go to men who are 100 per cent outside the family. The present chairman, Walter S. Carpenter, Jr., is in no way whatever a du Pont, but his oldest brother, Robert R., is married to a sister of Pierre S. du Pont, and his son Sam (general manager of the International Department) is likewise married to a du Pont. As for the current president — Crawford H. Greenewalt — his aunt is Mrs. William K. du Pont and he is also Irénée's son-in-law, and thus he is the nephew of Pierre S. both ways by marriage.

Needless to say, top positions in the company are not assigned solely on a basis of family membership, but the fact remains that up to now the family has been able to find competent people among its own ranks to take care of many important responsibilities in the company, thus serving the family's best interests, which by definition are also the stockholders'. The majority of the great American corporations have lost their family character. They have come under the diffuse control of masses of individual shareholders or of "communities" such as trust funds, mutual funds, colleges, insurance companies and syndicates. The administrative councils of these giant corporations are made up of professional businessmen who in thinking of their personal interests tend to forget the stockholders' interest. The democratic capitalist system is developing in some respects into a régime of irresponsible capitalism. Whether this system can continue to ward off socialism remains to be seen, particularly in view of the fact that under the pretext of avoiding the supposed danger represented by the power of great wealth, the United States government penalizes corporations which do too well.

It must be recognized that the Du Pont Company, by preserving family management as much as it could, is among those which have best resisted this tendency. The result, on the financial level, is perhaps worthy of note. In 1958 fifteen industrial corporations did a bigger business than Du Pont. But none of these made relatively so much profit. One of the very biggest made a net profit of only $526,475,000 on sales of $7,543,371,-000. Another made only $137,742,000 on sales of $2,005,837,000. But Du Pont made, on a business of only $1,825,250,000, a net gain of $341,248,000.

There are 31 members on the Du Pont board of directors, of whom nine are either du Ponts or du Pont relatives. It is this board which, meeting every month around the immense table in a room where inartistic portraits of all former presidents of E. I. Du Pont de Nemours line the walls, draws the company's main policy lines. All directors of the board have equal authority. The chairman presides at the meetings. However, practically speaking, the directors' authority is delegated to executive and finance committees, members of which are the happy few selected by the board from among its own membership. The finance committee holds the purse strings, and its decisions make the executive committee's proposals a reality, or not. There are only three du Ponts among the executive committee's total membership of nine, which meets every Wednesday in a room smaller than the one used by the whole board. However, there are five du Ponts, or du Pont relatives, on the eight-member finance committee. The company president, Crawford Greenewalt, belongs to both committees and acts also as adviser on public relations matters. Beyond this, two of the du Ponts who are directors are also board members, and again each one is a member of one of the committees. These same two du Ponts are also vice presidents of the company, and still another du Pont is company secretary. All three have key posts in the Christiana Securities Co. We must now talk a little about this company, since it holds the largest block of Du Pont de Nemours & Co. stock, and for this reason generally has the decisive vote at stockholders' meetings.

This holding company in September, 1958, by government estimate, had assets of $949,218,963. It is modestly housed in two small offices on the ninth floor of the Du Pont Building and employs only two men and one female secretary. In its portfolio Christiana has 12,199,200 shares of Du Pont, 535,500 of General Motors, and 8652 of Wilmington Trust. The Delaware Trust Company, meanwhile, has in its portfolio 43,500 shares of preferred and 49,000 shares of common stock of Christiana, giving it an incontestable control, plus 16,256 shares of Du Pont preferred and 1,217,920 of Du Pont common and 300,000 shares of Hercules Powder. The largest part of these securities stems from Coleman; they were bought by Pierre in 1915 for the syndicate's account. Christiana reports 3800 holders of common and 1410 of preferred stock. The Delaware Investment Trust has only 211 shareholders. At the top of the pyramid, holding the reins of command as president of this trust, is Lammot du Pont Copeland, assisted, among others, by Irénée du Pont, Jr., Pierre Samuel du Pont, III, Henry Belin du Pont and William K. du Pont Carpenter, all nephews of Pierre S. and all part inheritors of his great fortune.

At the beginning of 1961 it was decided that Delaware Investment would be absorbed into Christiana for tax reasons. Shareholders in Delaware Investment were being taxed twice on revenues coming in the form of dividends from the Christiana Securities Co. The Securities and Exchange Commission had a word to say about this merger operation, since the two companies, even if they were primarily a family affair, had had to be registered like any other closed end trust fund by virtue of the Investment Company Act of 1940. This metamorphosis in any case had little interest for small investors, since Christiana shares, even when they had been split 80 to 1, were worth $200 apiece — out of the reach of piggy-bank savers.

The Du Pont public relations department insists it does not know the name of the biggest single stockholder, but it would appear to be Lammot du Pont Copeland, son of Louise d'Andelot du Pont, sister of Pierre S., and Charles Copeland, who joined the company about 1903. He is fifty-seven years old and worked his way up through several Du Pont departments before being elected director and member of the board in 1942. Two years later he also became a member of the General Motors board, and held this position until 1959, at which time he was forced to resign because of the federal court action brought against Du Pont. His magnificent estate at Greenville, near Wilmington, was built after plans made by the well-known husband and wife architects, the Homseys. Mrs. Homsey's father was "Coly" du Pont's brother. Here, visitors of the caliber of the King of the Belgians and the Crown Prince of Greece have been regally entertained. One of their children, Mrs. James Biddle, has made a serious study of agriculture and is married to the associate curator in charge of the American Wing at the Metropolitan Museum of Art.

Pierre Samuel du Pont, III, Lammot's son, another nephew of Pierre S., lives in a château of the eighteenth-century delicate French style. This estate is named Bois des Fossés, after the château near Chevannes which once belonged to the illustrious ancestral Physiocrat. Pierre S., III, is company secretary, an important job, first, because he is in charge of company-stockholder relations — including relations with family stockholders — and second, because it is he who passes on reports of division heads relative to promotions. Since the company on occasion has almost fallen into the hands of strangers when management neglected to prepare teams of successors, the problem of forming managerial cadres has always loomed large in Du Pont thinking. But among the family, it appears, favoritism is reduced to a minimum, since it is to everybody's interest — the majority of employees own stock and top personnel are given stock for a bonus — not to entrust responsibility to incompetents. The division chiefs are masters in their own right. However, whenever they single out anyone as promising, he must still go through the mill. This company rule also applies to young du Ponts. For sixty years past not one of them has ever been given a top job without first having earned his spurs.

Irénée, Jr., only son of the octogenarian Irénée and brother of Mrs. Crawford Greenewalt, was elected to the board in 1959, after his father was no longer a member. Irénée is forty-two years old, with five children, and is often seen driving around Wilmington in an open antique automobile loaded with his family. From M.I.T., he entered the company in 1946. Irénée, Jr., is said to be the kind of du Pont who is presidential — that is, company presidential — timber.

Henry Belin du Pont, another nephew of Pierre (and son of Henry B. and Eleuthera Bradford du Pont), is also an M.I.T. graduate, as family tradition requires, but with the difference that he got his degree in 1923 in aeronautical engineering. It was undoubtedly this that led him to take an interest in the North American Aviation Company, which he serves as a director while also doubling in brass (since 1939) as a vice-president of E. I. Du Pont de Nemours and a member of the executive committee. A great lover of sport, he is widely known abroad as a yachtsman and owner of the 46-foot sloop *Cyane,* named for the flagship of Admiral Samuel Francis du Pont. He has also been commodore of the Cruising Club of America. His wife, née Emily du Pont, is 100 per cent one of the "du Pont ladies," for her great-great-grandfather was Victor, son of the Physiocrat.

We can round out our list of big company stockholders with William du Pont, Jr., a descendant of General Henry, sovereign of Du Pont de Nemours for so many years. William did not go to M.I.T. His chief interests in life are raising thoroughbred horses and the construction of race tracks. It is he who designed Delaware Park at Stanton, where every year big purse meets are held. William himself, according to the memorandum of Andrew Dallstream in the U.S. District Court in Illinois, owns 1,269,788 shares of Du Pont common. At 200 dollars a share, this makes him worth 301 million dollars. Beyond this, he owns a great deal of real estate in Wilmington and environs. After his divorce he married Miss Margaret Osborne of California, tennis champion of the international class.

Before World War II, correctly or not, the little town of Cognac was considered to be the richest in France,

if its total net worth were divided up among all inhabitants. Measured the same way, Wilmington is probably the richest town in America. Few cities of 100,000
in the United States have a legitimate theater, a race
track, four golf and tennis clubs, an airport and such
beautiful parks and museums. One of these last is the
Hagley Museum, built on the banks of the Brandywine
where the first powder mills of the Eleutherian Mills
were located. Some of these powder mills have been
preserved and are visited by school children and tourists, for whose benefit dioramas are shown, re-creating
the past. Those who are not satisfied with reproductions
and simulacra, and especially those interested in Ameri-
cana or period pieces of the American cultural heritage,
by applying well in advance can buy a ticket allowing
them to take part in one of the regular four-hour tours
of the Winterthur Museum.

Winterthur, named after Winterthur in Switzerland,
is located a short distance from Wilmington. It was
the home of Colonel Henry Algernon du Pont, and
before him the home of James-Antoine Bidermann,
who built it in 1837. Bidermann, of course, was the son-
in-law of Eleuthère-Irénée, founder of the Du Pont
Company. At enormous cost the house has been furnished with historic paintings and furniture. In 1951,
the Colonel's son, Henry Francis opened it to the public and beat a retreat to less encumbered lodgings, a
thirty-room "cottage." Four visitors at a time are led

through the house under a guide's vigilant eye. Among other things, they are shown over 100 period rooms, such as the Hart Room (furnished in the style of colonial Massachusetts in 1640), the Oyster Bay Room (1650 Long Island), Port Royal Parlor (1782 Philadelphia), Flock Room (1714 Virginia), and the Empire Room (1830 Albany). Great precautions are taken to make sure that the selected visitors do no damage. Canes, umbrellas and cameras must be left at the cloakroom, also ladies' handbags. Finally, the prospectus handed out to the public contains the following curious house rule, apparently indicating that strange people indeed sometimes penetrate this sanctuary of New World art: "Drinking of alcoholic beverages on the premises is prohibited." In Old World museums such as the Louvre, the Prado, the Vatican Museum, the Uffizi, the Parthenon, I have never read anything of the kind. But that, of course, is Henry Francis du Pont's affair! This publicity-shy gentleman, collector of beautiful things, recently got into the news when Jacqueline Kennedy, the President's wife, visited the Museum and selected him as an adviser on refurnishing the White House with period antiques.

One of the du Ponts told me that when he was still a student he was invited with a cousin of his own age to visit the Colonel at Winterthur, and after dinner incautiously decided to look through some of the rooms.

"It was all so big, so monstrously big, and there were

so many rooms, corridors and staircases that we got completely lost. Fortunately we found a telephone and called for help. We were asked what number station we were calling from and told not to budge from the spot until someone got there. . . . After some time a footman arrived. But he got lost, too, and called from another station to find out the route back to the drawing room, where the Colonel was playing bridge and had not even noticed our absence."

To the best of my knowledge, Henry F. is the only member of the family who has indulged so extensively in art objects. He carried this to such a point that he ended up with a museum instead of a livable home. None of the great du Pont ancestors who were contemporaries of Frick, Mellon, Pierpont Morgan, Whitney and Rockefeller were clients of Duveen, merchant of paintings for multimillionaires. I accept only with much reservation the story which tells how Alfred I., the "rebel," dickered and finally paid a high price for a supposed portrait of his great-grandmother, only to discover that it was a fake. But the surface paint having been removed, a masterpiece of another artist was disclosed beneath. Many du Pont homes are beautifully furnished, but not always with collector's items.

As for personal collections, Irénée specialized in minerals, Henry B. — the Navigator — in cannon models and marine engravings, Copeland in souvenirs of Lavoisier. Also there is Crawford Greenewalt's intense interest in hummingbirds, which has led to the publication of a best-selling book of photographs in color done by him.

And to mention a few interesting hobbies: Carita Ortiz Boden's "Kelso-Porsche Stable" of racing cars — Robert (or Bobby) Carpenter's absorption with the cellar-dwelling Phillies — Mrs. Philip du Pont's scrapbook for her mare which she, age eighty-eight, selected as the "daintiest." This same "Tempted" was chosen "mare of the year" in 1960 from 29,000 others. The most delightful hobby story concerns the elaborate barber chair placed in the bay window of the game room of one of the hospitable houses near Montchanin. It is there for the amusing lady of the house to trim the hair of any willing guest.

One passion shared by all du Ponts is for trees and flowers.

Among the du Ponts it is often emphasized that many members of the family are by no means as sumptuously rich as the ones we have just mentioned. Any number of du Pont relatives by marriage have positions of varying importance in any number of businesses, or are engaged in professions completely divorced from the Wilmington corporation. Among these du Ponts, for example, there are architects, lawyers, politicians, insurance brokers, bankers, real estate promoters, restaurant and shop owners, a movie director, an actress, any number of engineers, and finally gentlemen-farmers like Victor, great-great-grandson in direct line of the Physiocrat's oldest son Victor. A neighbor of President Kennedy, Victor farms near Middleburg, Virginia.

Among the most successful of this non-company group are Edmond and A. Rhett, sons of Francis I., who have done very well by building up the investment house founded by their father. Francis I. du Pont & Co. has become one of the largest investment firms in the U.S., with an affiliate in Switzerland. These two du Ponts are independent of the company although they do have a branch office in the Du Pont Building in Wilmington and one of their brothers, Emile, is a member of the board of E. I. du Pont de Nemours & Co.

I inquired of an older member of the family, "What, if any, is the influence of the du Pont women in your affairs?" He hesitated and then replied that by their French traditions, the place of women is in their homes. "We don't like," he added, "our women in business." Nevertheless, there seem now to be some exceptions. For example, there is Mrs. James Dean, who married into the William K. branch and who is co-owner of a dress shop. At Centerville, outside Wilmington, Mrs. Nicholas R. du Pont, internationally known beauty, is a partner in a boutique with the widow of Richard du Pont, who gave his life in the testing of gliders. In elegant competition to them, next door is the boutique of Mrs. Gordon A. Rust, née Frances du Pont. With the practical business instinct of her family, she has diversified "from gadgets to caviar and sables" with her personal chauffeur delivering all. Do these female ventures indicate a breakdown of the traditional deference to the wishes of the family elders? It lasted, anyway, for over 160 years.

On the political level the freedom of choice that is the rule in America also obtains among the du Ponts. Reynolds du Pont, son of Lammot, sits as a Republican in the Delaware Assembly, whereas his cousin Alexis I. du Pont Bayard, son of the Senator, is a pillar of the Democratic party. Occasionally called "traitors to their class," the Bayards characteristically ignore this. They are descended — according to tradition — from the famous French "chevalier without fear and without reproach," the sixteenth-century hero of King Francis I. Henry M. Baird, historian of Huguenot families in America, says that the common ancestor of these Bayards was a French Calvinist minister, Nicholas Bayard, who emigrated to America, and whose granddaughter Judith married Peter Stuyvesant, last governor of New Amsterdam. The du Ponts and the Bayards merged when a sister of the Philip du Pont who took Alfred's side in the "war of the du Pont clan" married the late Senator Thomas F. Bayard.

Left-wing New York publications at one time accused Pierre Samuel du Pont of having largely financed the Republican party's campaign chest to help elect Herbert Hoover President. Less widely known, however, is the fact that, disgusted with the prohibitionists, Pierre Samuel later went over into the opposite camp and joined forces with his friend and collaborator, John Raskob, in support of Al Smith. Again, to demonstrate political independence, about 1945 Miss Ethel D. du Pont, Coleman's niece, who lived in Kentucky, paid for pages of anti-General Motors publicity in the liberal *New Republic*.

What role do contemporary du Ponts play in Delaware politics? Like any shrewd businessmen, they can be on either side of the fence. It appears that recently the traditionally Republican, influential personalities in the company supported the re-election of the Democrat Frear, who lost the senatorial race, while backing the Republican Collins, running for governor, who also was beaten. From this we may conclude that in du Pont eyes men count more than party, if their company is to benefit, and also conclude that all the du Pont power is not sufficient to sway the voters of Delaware.

In this connection it may be recalled that in the days when businessmen generally considered the late President Franklin D. Roosevelt to be "an agent of Hell," a second Ethel du Pont, this one the daughter of Eugene, married the son of that "dreadful fellow," that "traitor to his class" — Franklin D., Jr. Scene of the wedding, naturally, was Christ Church, built in former times by Uncle Alexis Irénée.*

The President, apparently more delighted than the du Ponts with the match, was of course at the reception for the bride and groom. Undoubtedly he was surprised at what must have seemed to him to be a paucity of du Ponts in attendance. He probably never knew that many of them, not wanting to shake his hand, had put in an appearance by the back door to felicitate their cousin, and then, ignoring protocol, slipped out a back door to avoid what was later an incredible crush of traffic. It was reported backstairs that a pretty girl so captured the attention of the President that he remained at the party longer than was expected.

During this period in Wilmington, Christ Episcopal Church was better known as the "du Pont Church," for ever since it had been built, du Pont weddings and funerals had been held there. Recently, however, Christ Church lost its reputation for exclusiveness. Young women of the family about to get married now discover that the ceremony will have to be open to the public as in the case of common folks, and that only the ladies

* This church, the story goes, has the peculiarity of being, as it were, under the sign of whiskey. It so happened that Alexis Irénée arrived one day to look over the construction job, and happened to catch a mason, who had seen him coming, in the act of hiding among the stones of the wall a bottle of whiskey, from which he had just taken a swig. Pretending not to have noticed a thing, the implacable Alexis hung around until a reasonable number of stones had been sealed into place over the *corpus delicti*.

of the Altar Guild — not her friends, and definitely not
the professionals of the city's social affairs — will be allowed to arrange the secular details inside the church.

But the democratic attitude of this Episcopal church
will in no way affect, we need hardly say, the high
society role that the du Ponts play and will continue to
play in Delaware. Here the du Ponts are supremely
influential.

It seems to me as a Frenchman that no one is considered to have "arrived" in the United States until he
has been elected a member of the best local club and
has had his name put on the social list of the most
important families of the community. But it is difficult,
if not impossible, to define "Society" in America as it
can be categorized in Europe. At the same time, all
evidence indicates that such a Society does exist, with
its usual totems and taboos. Looked at from this angle,
Wilmington is not as snobbish, in the American sense,
as Boston or Philadelphia, but more so than New
York.

In Wilmington, members of the company management may call du Pont colleagues by their first names,
according to the established informality, and their
wives may meet du Pont women on charity committees,
at church affairs or debutante teas, but it does not
follow — and actually is far from being the case —
that such people are necessarily regularly invited to the

exclusive Vicmead Hunt Club or the du Pont debutante balls and family dinners. These coming-out balls for du Pont daughters, generally held in June or September, are magnificent affairs, framed by beautiful parks easy to transform for a night into an enchanted setting.

Such was an apple orchard, illuminated to imitate big red apples, on the approach to the ball for Carroll Morgan, now Mrs. John Gates. An acre of crystal décor, including chandeliers, was the spectacular achievement for the debut of Jane de Doliete du Pont, daughter of Pierre S., III. *Life* magazine covered this affair, which rivaled in beauty the great star-studded trees at the ball for her sister Michele. In the same year of 1959 Nicole du Pont (who joined the staff of *Vogue* magazine in 1961) made her debut at a lavish Bavarian-style ball.

The du Ponts cannot be lumped with the snobs and poseurs of society. Several family heirs have made surprising, democratic matches that have thrown Society back on its heels, but not one to my knowledge has ever swapped her inheritance for a resounding title like so many American women of wealth. In reverse of this, I have been told that some American men have come to Wilmington vowing not to leave until they had married a du Pont . . . and achieved this goal. One of the greatest French families, the Rohans, have this motto: *"Roi ne puis, Prince ne daigne, Rohan suis"* — "A king I can't be, a prince I wouldn't condescend to be, a Rohan I am." So, too, with the du Ponts. They are content with the name.

The du Ponts neither nourish any particular regard for crowned heads nor bestow much consideration on celebrities. Once, at a du Pont house, I was introduced to a young woman who was described to me simply as a compatriot Frenchwoman and the daughter of someone who had "written some books." I found that the girl's mother was Louise de Vilmorin, a woman of talent and author of novels famous everywhere, but Wilmington was unimpressed. On another occasion I met a "Mrs. Baviere" who I discovered was the royal princess of Bavaria. She had been left in a corner alone with her pretty daughter.

The du Ponts themselves are indifferent to what other people think of them. Whereas many rich New Yorkers of good family would be plunged into despair if their names were left out of the New York *Social Register*, of all the du Ponts who have a pied-à-terre in New York only one du Pont ménage, that of Henry F. of Winterthur, officially "belongs." His name is followed by a long series of letters indicating membership in such fashionable clubs as the Knickerbocker, National Golf, and Racquet, and his wife's by similar abbreviations for the Huguenot Society, the Colonial Dames of America, the Colony Club and the like. More numerous, on the other hand, are the du Ponts listed in the Philadelphia

Social Register, for the reason that this book includes Wilmington.

Need I add that the du Ponts seem to have little inclination to mingle with the mob of the *Who's Who in America,* that monumental dictionary of accomplishment which runs to over 3300 large pages printed in small type. One can say correctly that these people have a simple dislike of *nouveau riche* ostentation. If not many du Ponts ride in chauffeur-driven Rolls-Royces, Bentleys, Daimlers, or Mercedes, but rather in Cadillacs, often venerable ones, or in Oldsmobiles, Chevrolets or even in Corvairs, it is quite certain that they do it for the sake of remaining inconspicuous, and not, as would be natural, to prosper General Motors, which used to be about 23 per cent theirs.

As an indication of what the du Ponts are *not,* a certain show girl from Long Island who married into the family might be cited. Her first acquisition was a white Rolls-Royce, the better to show off her black hair, gray eyes and fair skin. Lunching one day with her new cousins, they asked where she had come out. "Right out of Tiffany's window," she quipped and, with no inhibitions about *nouveau riche* ostentation, she extended an arm loaded with giant diamonds. But she is no longer in the family.

I have remarked that the personal affairs of the family are absolutely never discussed outside the du Pont circle. It has been rare that scandals have escaped these bounds. It would take endless pages to recount all the anecdotes, chitchat and idle talk, nor would they have much bearing. I repeat only in passing the droll story of the cocktail guests who lingered in a du Pont garden until dark. A light appeared upstairs and they watched, in laughter, the loving but ever-absent-from-such-affairs husband of their hostess, drip-drying his nylon shorts.

Also there was this tragicomic story told me about a picturesque du Pont assigned to Cleveland years ago by the company. This charming fellow was a great drinker. Being bored by long trips, he found distraction on a train that was taking him back to grim duty at the Wilmington headquarters by consuming several bottles of whiskey. Indeed, he drank so much that, feeling fatigued, he got off the train at the first convenient stop along the route. He still had enough presence of mind to get himself taken by taxi to the "best hotel," where he could get a good night's rest before showing up in Wilmington. Being no new hand at this caper, he bethought himself to leave an order at the desk to have the local paper sent up in the morning, an easy way of finding out just what city he was in. The local paper turned out to be the Pittsburgh *Press,* with a big headline saying: "Train Catastrophe, a du Pont among the Victims!" The train which he had so opportunely left had had a terrible accident. A forgotten piece of his luggage having been found in one of the wrecked cars the night before, he had been listed among the dead. Brought up sharp by this news of his tragic end, our hero telegraphed his wife: "I am all right. Will return this evening from Pittsburgh. Stopped off to take care of some important business." He was welcomed home with expressions of great joy. Nobody in his family, however, was the least taken in. But secretly everyone was delighted that, for this once, his intemperate habits had saved his life.

And perhaps I should not repeat the reply I got from one of the prettiest girls in the family when I asked her, after she had visited Paris for the first time, how she had liked Notre Dame. To this she said: "Oh, I didn't really need to go there. I could see it just as well from the Tour d'Argent where my parents had reserved the best table by the window for dinner."

Epilogue

IN ALL OBJECTIVITY, it must be said that the du Pont family, by migrating to the United States, found the most favorable climate for amply ensuring their children's welfare. And that with all the revolutions, wars and currency devaluations, they would have been hard put to accumulate and keep such a fortune in Europe in general and France in particular.

Pierre-Samuel, the Physiocrat, whose motto was *Aimer et connaître* (Love and understand), wrote in his *Philosophie de l'Univers:*

> The mild and moderate, judicious and republican government of the United States offers almost the only asylum where the persecuted may find repose, where fortunes may be reborn through toil, where the head of the family through prudence may set aside a reserve, a last storehouse to ensure his children's sustenance. . . .

The success story of the family of du Pont de Nemours, unique in America or in the world, has certainly borne him out.

Bibliography

Aimé, Denise, *Du Pont de Nemours, honnête homme* (Paris, 1934).

Arey, H. W., *The Girard College and Its Founder* (Philadelphia, 1860).

Baird, Charles W., *Histoire des Huguenots d'Amérique* (Paris, 1812).

Baudin, Louis, *Précis d'histoire des doctrines économiques* (Paris, 1947).

Bayard, Thomas, *Oration Delivered at the Unveiling of the Statue of Samuel Francis du Pont* (Washington, 1885).

Biot, Jean-Baptiste, *Essai sur l'histoire générale des sciences pendant la Révolution* (Paris, 1803).

Blanc, Louis, *Histoire de la Révolution* (Paris, 1847-1862).

Chaumartin, Henri, *F. Quesnay* (Paris, 1936).

Clayton, J. M., *Speech in Regard to Captain S. F. Du Pont* (Washington, 1856).

Daire, Eugène, *Physiocrates* (Paris, 1846).

Du Bin, Alexander, *Canby, Shipley, Lea, Roberts, Price, Bradford, Du Pont, Boden, Newkirk Families* (Philadelphia, 1951).

Dujarric de la Rivière, *E. I. du Pont de Nemours, élève de Lavoisier* (Paris, 1954).

du Pont, Bessie Gardner, *E. L. du Pont de Nemours and Company; A History, 1802-1902* (Wilmington, 1920).

——, *Life of E. I. du Pont* (12 vols., Wilmington, 1923-1927).

——, *Lives of Victor and Josephine du Pont* (Greenville, Delaware, 1930).

[291]

du Pont, Francis I., *The Chemical Industry* (New York, 1936).

du Pont, Henry Algernon, *Rear Admiral Samuel F. du Pont* (New York, 1920).

————, *The Early Generations of the du Pont and Allied Families* (New York, 1923).

du Pont, Josephine (Mme. Victor du Pont), *Notre transplantation en Amérique* (unpublished; 1826; Eleutherian Mills Historical Library).

————, *Souvenirs* (Wilmington, 1908).

du Pont, Pierre-Samuel, *Réflexions sur l'écrit intitulé: Richesse de l'état* (Paris, 1763).

————, *De l'exportation et de l'importation des grains* (Paris, 1764).

————, *Table raisonnée des Principes d'Economie politique* (Carlsruhe, 1775).

————, *Mémoires sur la Vie et les Ouvrages de M. Turgot, ministre d'état* (Paris, 1782).

————, *Idées sur les secours à donner aux pauvres malades dans une grande ville* (Paris, 1786).

————, *Discours prononcé à l'Assemblée Nationale sur les banques en général et la Caisse d'escompte en particulier* (Paris, 1789).

————, *De la manière la plus favorable d'effectuer les emprunts* (Paris, 1789).

————, *De la meilleure manière de délibérer et de voter dans une grande assemblée* (Paris, 1789).

————, *Considérations sur la position politique de la France, de l'Angleterre et de l'Espagne* (Paris?, 1790?).

————, *De l'étendue et des bornes naturelles du droit de tester* (Paris, 1790).

————, *Opinion de M. Du Pont, deputé de Nemours, sur le projet de créer pour dix neuf cents millions d'assignats-monnoie* (Paris, 1790).

————, *Adresse aux français* (Paris, 1792).

————, *Avant-dernier chapitre de l'Histoire des Jacobins* (Paris, 1792).

————, *Traité d'Alliance offensive entre les français émigrants-aristocrates d'une part et les français républicains d'autre part* (Paris, 1792).

————, *Vues sur l'éducation nationale, par un cultivateur* (Paris, An II).

————, *Du pouvoir législatif et du pouvoir exécutif convenables à la république française* (Paris, An III).

————, *De l'influence et de l'utilité des clubs* (Attributed to P. S. du Pont, Paris, An IV).

————, *Compagnie d'Amérique, Mémoire qui contient le plan des opérations de la société* (Paris, An VII).

————, *Philosophie de l'Univers* (Paris, An VIII).

————, *Doutes et préventions relativement à la restitution à faire aux propriétaires américains du navire le New Jersey* (Paris?, 1804?).

————, *Sur l'éducation nationale dans les Etats-Unis d'Amérique* (Paris, 1812).

————, *L'enfance et la jeunesse de Du Pont de Nemours racontées par lui-même* (Paris, 1906).

————, *Un épilogue du 9 Thermidor: Lettres de Du Pont de Nemours écrites de la prison de la Force et publiées par G. Chinard* (Paris, 1929).

————, *Irénée Bonfils sur la religion de ses pères et de nos pères*, translated by Pierre S. du Pont (Wilmington, 1947).

————, ed., *Ephémérides du Citoyen, ou Bibliothèque raisonnée des sciences morales et politiques* (Paris, 1765-1772). Edited by Pierre-Samuel du Pont de Nemours from May, 1768, to November, 1772.

du Pont, Thomas Coleman, *A Constructive Businessman* (Boston, 1910).

————, *The High Cost of Living and Its Relation to the Distribution of Farm Products and Good Market Roads* (Boston, 1916).

Du Pont de Nemours, E. I., & Co., *High Explosives* (Wilmington, 1911).

————, *Blasters Handbook* (Wilmington, 1922).

————, *The Du Pont Company and Munitions* (Wilmington, 1934).

————, *Duprene: A Story of Man Made Rubber* (Wilmington, 1934).

————, *Explosives: Their Significance, Manufacture, and Use* (Wilmington, n.d.).

Du Pont de Nemours: Photos Collected by Louise d'Andelot du Pont Copeland (n.p., 1937).

Dutton, W. S., *Du Pont: One Hundred and Forty Years* (New York, 1942).

Fountains of Longwood Gardens (Longwood Foundation, 1960).

Gareschè, Louis, *Biography of Lieutenant Colonel Julius P. Gareschè, by His Son* (Philadelphia, 1887).

Genealogy of the Du Pont Family, 1739-1942 (Wilmington, 1943).

Gore, Walter, *History of the Barksdale, Du Pont and Allied Families* (New York, 1922).

Greenewalt, C. H., *The Uncommon Man* (New York, 1959).

Hatch, Alden, *Remington Arms in American History* (New York, 1956).

Héline, Maxime, *La Poudre à canon* (Paris, 1877).

Henry, Allan J., *The Life of Alexis Irénée du Pont* (Philadelphia, 1945).

Highlights of Wilmington, 1832-1932 (Charter Centennial Commission, 1932).

Holbrook, Stewart, *The Age of the Moguls* (New York, 1953).

Jennings, W. J., *A Dozen Captains of American Industry* (New York, 1953).

Keating, L. C., *Les Du Pont* (New York, 1959).

Kerr, George, *Du Pont Romance* (Wilmington, 1936).

Lacour-Gayet, *Talleyrand* (Paris, n.d.).

Lawton, W. C., *The Du Ponts: A Case Study of Kinship in the Business Organization* (Chicago, 1955).

Mackey, A. Gallatin, *The History of Freemasonry* (copyrighted 1898 and 1905 by the Masonry Historic Co., New York, London).

Macklenn, William, *Sixty Years of Du Pont Lodge No. 29 Ancient Free and Accepted Masons* (Wilmington, 1939).

Marquis, James, *Alfred du Pont, the Family Rebel* (New York, 1941).

Memorial of Charles Irénée du Pont (Wilmington, 1869).

Montchanin, *Notice sur la vie de Du Pont* (Paris, 1818).

Montgomery, Elizabeth, *Reminiscences of Wilmington* (Wilmington, 1851).

Pilon, Edmond, "Le Roman de Mme Poivre" (*Revue des Deux Mondes*, Paris, 1933).

Quinn, T. K., *Giant Business: Threat to Democracy* (New York, 1953).

Raskob, John J., *Green Record Book* (Claymont, Delaware, 1921).

————, *Last Will and Testament* (New York, 1950?).

Reed, H. Clay, *Delaware: A History of the First State* (New York, 1947).

Schelle, G., *Du Pont de Nemours et l'Ecole Physiocratique* (Paris, 1888).

Sédillot, René, *Survol de l'histoire de France* (Paris, 1958?).

Silliman, Charles A., *The Story of Christ Church Christiana Hundred and Its People* (Greenville, Delaware, 1961).

Spécialités de la Maison (published by the American Friends of France, 1940).

United States District Court for the Northern District of Illinois, *Opinion of Judge Walter La Buy* (Chicago, 1954).

————, *Report and Recommendations of Andrew J. Dallstream* (August 1958).

Whitney, Simon S., *Antitrust Policies* (New York, 1958).

Wilson, James G., *Colonel James J. Bayard and the Bayards of America* (New York, 1885).

Winkler, J. D., *The Du Pont Dynasty* (New York, 1935).

Woelmar, Baron de, *La Noblesse subsistante.*

Yost, Stan, *The Great Old Cars: Where Are They Now?* (Mendota, Illinois, 1960).

Index

Index